BAND OF SISTERS

BAND OF SISTERS

Madeleine Pauliac, the Women of the Blue Squadron, and Their Daring Rescue Missions in the Last Days of World War II

Philippe Maynial

Translated from the French by Richard Bernstein

ROWMAN & LITTLEFIELD
Lanham • Boulder • New York • London

Published by Rowman & Littlefield
An imprint of The Rowman & Littlefield Publishing Group, Inc.
4501 Forbes Boulevard, Suite 200, Lanham, Maryland 20706
www.rowman.com

86-90 Paul Street, London EC2A 4NE

Distributed by NATIONAL BOOK NETWORK

British Library Cataloguing in Publication Information Available

Library of Congress Cataloging-in-Publication Data

Names: Maynial, Philippe, author. | Bernstein, Richard, 1944- translator.
Title: Band of sisters : Madeleine Pauliac, the women of the Blue
   Squadron, and their daring rescue missions in the last days of
   World War II / Philippe Maynial ; translated from the French by
   Richard Bernstein.
Other titles: Madeleine Pauliac, the women of the Blue Squadron,
   and their daring rescue missions in the last days of World War II
Description: Lanham : Rowman & Littlefield, [2025] | Includes index.
Identifiers: LCCN 2024041805 (print) | LCCN 2024041806 (ebook) |
   ISBN 9781538198797 (cloth) | ISBN 9781538198803 (epub)
Subjects: LCSH: World War, 1939-1945—Underground
   movements—France—Biography. | World War, 1939-1945—Civilian
   relief—Poland. | World War, 1939-1945—Search and rescue
   operations—Soviet Union. | Croix-Rouge francaise—Biography. |
   Pauliac, Madeleine, 1912-1946. | Women physicians—France—
   Biography. | World War, 1939-1945—Medical care—Poland. |
   World War, 1939-1945—Poland—Forced repatriation. | World War,
   1939-1945—Prisoners and prisons.
Classification: LCC D802.F8 P37556 2025 (print) | LCC D802.F8 (ebook) |
   DDC 940.5344092 [B]—dc23/eng/20240906
LC record available at https://lccn.loc.gov/2024041805
LC ebook record available at https://lccn.loc.gov/2024041806

♾™ The paper used in this publication meets the minimum requirements
of American National Standard for Information Sciences—Permanence of
Paper for Printed Library Materials, ANSI/NISO Z39.48-1992

CONTENTS

PROLOGUE

She was an invisible presence. In words, in memories, in a time that wasn't my own, I kept hearing about a woman who wasn't there. As a child, I'd listen to adults talk about her, as if her presence were obvious, palpable, sovereign, and yet she was a ghost. I knew nothing about Madeleine Pauliac, except that she was my aunt and that she was a hero. As soon as her name was mentioned, an atmosphere of respect asserted itself, and in the family home, the terrible fate she suffered was suddenly pushed away, such that Madeleine emerged through the conversation about her with her dignity intact, and I would go back to my games, without worrying any more about her. For a little boy, the past is just a thing without weight, and the war, which was still on everyone's lips, seemed far away to me, situated in a universe that I vaguely sensed existed before I was born.

When my mother spoke of her sister in those immediate postwar years, she always used the word *admirable*. Madeleine, yes, had been admirable, but complicated feelings, streams of love, waves of regret, were hidden behind that word. There was sadness and affection, respect, and compassion. My mother, Anne-Marie Pauliac-Maynial, never pronounced the name of her departed sister without a kind of devotion mingled with nostalgia.

Figure 0.1 Madeleine, on the left, and my mother, Anne-Marie, who never mentioned her disappeared sister's name without a sort of devotion mixed with nostalgia. Madeleine was dead, to be sure, but for Anne-Marie, she was always there.

The two Pauliac sisters grew up in Villeneuve-sur-Lot, population twenty-two thousand, on the edge of the Périgord region in Southwest France, northwest of Toulouse, southeast of Bordeaux. It was, and remains, a picturesque place whose stately mansions date to the thirteenth century. It has a medieval-era church, open-air cafés on the town square, and a thirteenth-century arched stone bridge over the Lot River—along with a more recent span called the Bridge of the Liberation, completed just after World War I. It's beautiful country in what's sometimes called La France profonde, the remote provinces where family roots go back centuries and agriculture has always been the main industry. The Lot River flowed into the Garonne five hundred kilometers away, its meandering through the countryside resembling the calligraphy of the gods. My maternal grandfather ran a canning factory in Villeneuve. The factory employed around a hundred workers. Life was regulated by the harvests—plums, strawberries, tomatoes, and beans. I spent all my vacations in my grandfather's large manor house at 15, rue d'Agen. From my room, I could see the immense garden stretching as far as the fairgrounds. From the house, I could watch the workers, who unloaded tomatoes and plums from trucks that arrived in the dark at 4 a.m. Dawn would break over red stains on the ground. The tomatoes had bled, their juice ran into the gutters, the whole street turned crimson, and the smell of tomatoes filled the air.

With the trucks gone and the men back at the cannery, all that remained was that sweet fragrance wafting through the cool morning air, transforming the neighborhood into a market gardener's bouquet. The tomato massacres left their mark on my childhood as they no doubt did on Madeleine's.

Perhaps this vegetable blood foretold what would happen in other lands marked by the blood of men.

Madeleine and Anne-Marie's father, Roger Pauliac, was mobilized in 1914. He never saw his daughters again, Anne-Marie, who was two years old, and Madeleine, only one. He was mowed down along with thousands of other unfortunates in the forest of Avocourt at the start of the Battle of Verdun in March 1916, under a deluge of German 210 mm shells. All that remains today is a large painting of him in his midshipman's uniform adorned with his two military medals. All his daughters knew of their father, swallowed up by the turmoil of history, was this two-square-meter portrait in oil, which showed him posed nobly in profile, an image of dignity and distance.

In 1939, when the storm was brewing once again, Madeleine was twenty-seven years old. She was a bright, determined young woman who had completed her medical studies and was working at the Hôpital des Enfants-Malades, the Hospital for Sick Children, in Paris. Germany conquered France in 1940, and Madeleine joined the Resistance while working as a doctor in Paris, with a specialty in emergency pediatric tracheostomies. After France was liberated but with several months of the war still to be fought, she undertook a mission, ordered by Charles de Gaulle, the head of France's provisional government, to find and rescue French citizens who had become trapped in enemy territory, most of it now controlled by the Russian Red Army, and repatriate them to France. After a few months, she was joined by a task force of eleven young nurses and ambulance drivers who followed the American army in Germany seeking French soldiers who were trapped in hospitals and camps, treating them medically and bringing them back to France. After their job in Germany was finished, these women, young, intrepid, unstoppable, known as the Blue Squadron after the color of their American-donated uniforms, crossed the border into Poland, and for the next four months helped Madeleine to carry out a similar, but much more hazardous, mission there. Madeleine, a few years older and the only fully qualified medical doctor among them, became both their soulmate and their leader.

"The ambulances crisscrossed all of Poland, East Prussia, and Pomerania," Madeleine wrote in a report on the mission. "They made three incursions into Soviet territory; they drove 40,000 kilometers [25,000 miles] altogether. About 1,450 men were brought back, including many from Alsace and Lorraine. Two hundred missions were accomplished."

After reporting to Charles de Gaulle himself, Madeline could have stayed in France, which is what all the women of the Blue Squadron did, embarking on normal lives, working, marrying, having children and grandchildren. She chose instead to return to Poland in February 1946. She died soon afterward, on the thirteenth of that month, in an overloaded embassy car, along an icy road at the end of Eastern Europe.

She'd gone back to Soviet-occupied Poland to satisfy some need, incited by the devastation she'd seen there, the wounded children, the women raped and humiliated, to continue what she'd started, even though helping the local population wasn't part of her official mission. Poland, now being forced into the Soviet orbit, haunted her. She gave it her life.

Figure 0.2   The portrait of Roger Pauliac, who died in combat in March 1916 at Verdun during World War I. Madeleine and Anne-Marie grew up without him, but he remained a hero to both of them all their lives.

After all these years, I still didn't know much about her. Madeleine was the absence at family gatherings, spoken of with reverence, but with no real shape or form. Until, in 2006, shortly before my mother died, she entrusted me with an envelope, containing a few photos and letters from her sister, a logbook, and some reports. She said to me, "That's all that's left."

Perhaps it was when my mother died, a very painful moment for me, that the desire to bring Madeleine to life imposed itself. I began writing down the little I'd heard about her, rummaging through archives, sifting through yellowed statements, articles, and reports that crumbled under my fingers. I gathered these scattered elements. I dug into the historical archives; I learned about some of the missions, the more hair-raising of them, the subterfuges the Blue Squadon used to distract obstructionist Russian and Polish communist soldiers, their terror of being raped themselves, their confrontations with the evil they saw in concentration camps, their warding off the attentions of drunken commanders, the breakdowns on narrow, pockmarked roads when suddenly in the middle of the night the air filter on one of their Austin ambulances was flooded with motor oil. Most poignant of all, and perhaps the reason for Madeleine's return to Poland, was that, according to my mother, Madeleine had been involved in creating an orphanage near Warsaw to help lost and abandoned children, and children "did come," born as the result of the rape of nuns. Not only did she care for the pregnant nuns, with the utmost discretion, but she also set up a home for the newborns, where they, along with other orphans, were able to survive.

This story of the secret orphanage was the basis for a feature film, *Les Innocentes*, directed by Anne Fontaine. It played in theaters in 2016 (and can be seen still on Amazon Prime Video). But the film tells only a small part of the story of Madeleine and the Blue Squadron as they sought to rescue French nationals who were in the wrong place as World War II came to its brutal finale in Germany and Eastern Europe.

For me, finally, the time had come to meet my mysterious, heroic aunt, dead all those years before. I felt the need to tell as full a story as I could of this band of twelve brave sisters, Madeleine and the Blue Squadron, a story hardly known even in their native France, much less elsewhere in the world.

Their collective portrait is inseparable from the very particular historical conditions that prevailed at the end of the war in the territories where Madeleine, the nurses, and the ambulance drivers worked. Given the Russian presence in Poland at the time and the conflict between communists and non-communist Poles, the political stakes were high, and it was impossible for the members of the French women's expedition to avoid the reality on the ground as they pursued their mission. There was a violence, a barbarity, that drew the women, especially Madeleine, into an activism that lay beyond their official instructions and that left its mark on them all.

In addition to my mother's confidences, I was fortunate to receive those of the last witness to this period still alive, Simone Saint-Olive, known as "Sainto," one of the Blue Squadron nurses.

And so, little by little, the impressive yet evanescent silhouette that accompanied my childhood took shape, became denser. By reconstructing Madeleine's life and the key episodes of her mission in the East, I got to know an extraordinary woman, lively, intelligent, determined, with a character of astonishing strength and courage, a person who left an indelible mark on the men and women who met her, and on me, her nephew, who is meeting her now in the pages of this book.

Chapter 1

SO FAR FROM PARIS

(March 28–April 7, 1945)

I've wondered what Madeleine was thinking as she flew over the Egyptian pyramids and the Sphinx, with its severed nose, on her roundabout route to Warsaw. What could have been on the mind of a young female medical doctor, leaving her family, her country, for an assignment she knew was going to be dangerous? It must have been strange, seeing the pyramids from the air, almost dreamlike, so far from home and, in every conceivable way, alien, especially in light of her fraught destination.

Madeleine was a kind of ward of the French nation brought up to idolize a father who "died for France." This inscription can be seen on the thousands of memorials found all over France, in every town and village, to the soldiers of World War I who never came back from the battlefields. Perhaps because of her reverence for her father, and her country, Madeleine had always taken her own, unconventional route, not absolutely unique for women in the France of that time, but unusual, showing an independence of spirit that became widespread only decades later, establishing herself in a profession before thinking of starting a family. Her sister, my mother, chose the more conventional route, marrying and producing children once her studies ended.

Both sisters went to a lycée, the French equivalent of high school, in the Mediterranean coast city of Nice, where they lived with their mother. After graduating, their paternal grandmother sent them to Paris and rented an apartment for them on the Avenue Bosquet, near the Military Academy. That's where Madeleine went to medical school,

Figure 1.1 The two sisters, Anne-Marie and Madeleine (right in the picture), were brought up in a traditionally religious household (here the day of their first communion), but Madeleine's faith was deeply shaken by what she experienced during the war in her rescue mission in Poland.

quickly deciding to specialize in pediatrics. When she completed her qualifications, she was admitted into the Ordre des Médecins, France's professional accreditation for doctors, giving her the right to practice medicine. At that time, she was one of only 350 Frenchwomen in France to have achieved that distinction.

Figure 1.2 After achieving her high school diploma, Madeleine studied medicine in Paris, getting her degree in 1939 just when World War II was beginning in Europe, becoming one of just 350 women admitted to the Ordre des Médecins, France's professional accreditation for doctors. She was twenty-seven.

Then came World War II and the sudden, shocking defeat of France. The German occupation began, abruptly, in May 1940. At the Hospital for Sick Children, Madeleine had to cope with shortages and restrictions. She learned to deprive herself. Whenever I look at photographs of my aunt from that period, I'm struck by her youthfulness and the strength that seems to emanate from her image. She poses with a hint of a smile on her lips, looking straight ahead. She always knew what she wanted!

She took part in the resistance, outside of the hospital, outside of Paris, taking chances. In 1947, she received the Légion d'Honneur, posthumously, the citation recognizing "her activity and devotion in the service of the resistance, undertaking, despite the danger, the resupply of the maquis where she brought medical help to allied parachutists," dropped into France, usually at night, by the British and the Americans. My mother used to tell me that Madeleine even lodged some of these men where she lived, on the ground floor of a building with a small garden at 59 Boulevard Beauséjour, in the 16th arrondissement of Paris. But as far as we know, Madeleine mainly continued to fulfill her duties at the hospital, the world's first pediatric hospital, founded in 1802 on the rue de Sèvres in Paris, where she performed the tricky procedure of inserting breathing tubes through the necks of small children. She also took part in the liberation of Paris, which happened on August 26, 1944, when Allied troops, led by a contingent of French soldiers under General Charles de Gaulle, marched into the city. Madeleine no doubt shared the eruption of joy that accompanied the liberation; perhaps she was among the huge throngs that danced in the streets or lined the Champs Elysées to greet the arriving Allied troops.

But while Paris was free, there was still so much to do elsewhere. The war was not over. The Americans, British, and Canadians were advancing into Germany from the west; the Soviets, having fought their way through Poland, from the east. Madeleine signed up as a medical lieutenant, registration number 44-758 027 00, on November 30, 1944, meaning that she was now a soldier in the French army. During that frigid winter, she participated in the campaigns to liberate the Vosges region and Alsace, which were among the most deadly of the actions in all of the war—seventy-six thousand American soldiers dead, wounded, or missing in action, against sixty-seven thousand Germans, among whom were battle-hardened SS divisions that had seen action against Russian troops on the eastern front.

De Gaulle, who had headed the French government in exile during the war, was now the head of a provisional government that would rule the newly liberated country until elections could be held. At some point in the early spring of 1945, he summoned Medical Lieutenant Pauliac, now thirty-two years old, to a meeting, almost certainly at the Ministry of War on the rue Saint-Dominique in Paris. Among her qualifications, she was unmarried; without children; a woman of an engaged, independent character; and the child of a man who had "died for France" at Verdun. She had seen action as a medical officer, so she knew how to treat wounded men under harsh conditions, and where she was going, there would be harsh conditions and plenty of wounded men to treat.

The political situation was complex, tense, messy, with many problems left over from the war years that had yet to be decided. When France surrendered to Germany in 1940, it was divided into two zones, one of them comprising the northern half of the country and the Atlantic coast, which fell under direct German occupation. The second part, the southern half of the country, was technically independent, with a government based in the French resort city of Vichy, supposedly running its own affairs, but in fact collaborating with the Nazis. A few leaders, de Gaulle most notably, saw through this fiction and rejected the country's capitulation, going first to London, then, after the Allies took over North Africa from the Germans, to Algiers, which became the headquarters of the Free French forces. When the Allied forces liberated Paris in August 1944, troops from the Free French army were allowed to be the first to enter the city.

But from the surrender of 1940 until Paris's liberation four years later, the Vichy government, led by the aging Marshal Philippe Pétain, who had been a hero of World War I, essentially put all of France at the service of Germany, adopting its antiliberal, antidemocratic, and antisemitic ideology, replacing France's national motto, *Liberté, Egalité, Fraternité*—Liberty, Equality, Fraternity—with a new authoritarian idea summed up in the slogan *Travail, Famille, Patrie*—Work, Family, Homeland.

When it defeated the French army in 1940, Germany took some two million French soldiers as prisoner, and when France was liberated, a substantial number of these soldiers, though technically "liberated" by the Russians, were still in camps in Germany, Poland, and even in some parts of the Soviet Union.

Others, the so-called *malgré-nous*, meaning literally, "despite ourselves," from the provinces of Alsace and Lorraine, bordering Germany, had been conscripted into the Wehrmacht on August 23, 1942, and forced to fight against their will, so that when they were defeated and taken prisoner, some by the Americans, others on the eastern front by the

Russians, they were wearing German uniforms and were unable to prove that they were French. But they were nonetheless entitled to be allowed to return to their homes. In addition, tens of thousands of French citizens had been drafted into the Service de Travail Obligatoire, or STO, the Forced Labor Service, and had been sent to farms or factories in Germany or German-occupied Poland to replace Germans who had left for the front. There were also some French, following the collaborationist policies of the Vichy regime, who volunteered to fight on Germany's side during the war. These included members of the paramilitary militias, created in the unoccupied zone of France to serve as a kind of private army for the Vichy regime, searching for resistance fighters and other enemies.

When the war ended, many of the French nationals in Poland and other countries in the East made it quickly back to France, generally after being shipped to the Black Sea port of Odessa, from which they boarded boats to the French Mediterranean port of Marseille. But a large number of them, estimated by de Gaulle himself to be five hundred thousand, were being held in various camps in Poland or in Russia itself, many of them sick or wounded, getting rudimentary, primitive care in undersupplied and undermanned Polish or Soviet hospitals, with no way on their own to get back to France. "They were scattered haphazardly, without leadership, without connections, in the entire extent of the ravaged country," a diplomat assigned by de Gaulle to handle negotiations with local communist authorities wrote later. "Our worries weren't limited to the physical health of our compatriots, their food and clothing. We also thought that if they were grouped together only by the Soviets, tired of being rounded up again, they would foment violent incidents. . . . Others, by contrast, weakened by their captivity, cut off from their country, would be indoctrinated ideologically by their liberators and would enroll in the [communist] Party."

The French even supposed that some of these soldiers would form themselves into a French force wearing Soviet uniforms that Moscow could keep in reserve, permanently lost to France. It was urgent, therefore, that French teams make contact with as many of them as possible as soon as possible, but they also knew that the Russians, though they agreed in principle to their repatriation, wouldn't do much to help the French find their compatriots and were even likely to obstruct the effort.

In December 1944, just three months after the Germans withdrew from Paris, de Gaulle himself had gone to Moscow, where he negotiated with Stalin over the repatriation of the liberated French prisoners in Russia and Poland; he'd also named two diplomats, Francois Huré and Christian Fouchet, to take charge of the mission in Poland. And he ordered Madeleine, a medical doctor and an officer in the French army, to join the Warsaw task force.

"We must go to Russia, then Poland," de Gaulle had told Madeleine. "There are more than half a million French people there, who need to be repatriated as quickly as possible." De Gaulle's estimate was on the high side, but even the low estimate of three hundred thousand was a large number.

And that brings us to the airplane flying over Egypt, bringing Madeleine toward her mission in the heavily war-scarred northeastern front of the war.

She had left Le Bourget, then Paris's main airport, on March 28. General Alphonse Juin, who had commanded de Gaulle's French Expeditionary Corps in North Africa and in the invasion of Italy, came to greet her before takeoff. The flight gave Madeleine her last glimpses of the city where she had lived since the early 1930s, the Arc de Triomphe, Trocadéro, Les Invalides. The plane flew southeast over the beautiful French countryside, just starting to thaw out from winter.

I can just imagine her: Madeleine jots down notes as she flies over cities devastated by the wartime bombing—Bourges, Montluçon, Tulle. Her long hair is tied back, and she wears her military uniform; she looks down on the France for which she still wants to fight. The roundabout route the plane takes is necessary to avoid overflying the zones in Germany and Central Europe, where the war is still raging. But to be out of France up in the sky, watching the landscape below, must have been exhilarating after being locked in the heart of Paris in the midst of war for five long years, with its ration coupons and curfews and German soldiers in the cafés and the streets.

The plane makes several stopovers for fuel and sleep before heading out over the Mediterranean and then to Egypt, where they land. Madeleine is struck by the abundance she sees in Cairo, so different from what she'd gotten used to in France. "There's everything: doughnuts, pastries, fruit, strawberries, oranges, bananas, lemons." Cairo strikes

Madeleine, who had never left France before, as cosmopolitan, teeming, and exotic.

After Cairo, the plane flies over the Suez Canal, Tel Aviv, and Acre—Akko in Israel today—where she can see the old citadel, and she remembers from some long-ago history lesson that that was the place where, in 1799, Napoleon's campaign to control the entire Middle East came to an end at the hands of the Turks. She also knows that Acre was the starting point for the Sykes-Picot Agreement of 1916, which, anticipating the disintegration of the Ottoman Empire, divided up the Middle East into British and French zones of influence. There's a stopover in Beirut, and the next day, Madeleine's plane flies over the mountains of Lebanon on the way to Damascus—"a yellow desert with forests, cliffs." She sees the Euphrates River and Baghdad on the way to the next stopover, Tehran and its oil wells. As they head north, the weather deteriorates, and the last stop before the departure for Moscow is in Astrakhan, on the shores of the Caspian Sea, in the middle of a storm.

General Georges Catroux, De Gaulle's representative in Moscow, had a reputation for always being gloomy, always looking gray—that's how he was portrayed by people who knew him at the time as well as by historians today. Certainly, he faced a difficult situation in Moscow, which, as he had quickly discovered, was not a welcoming place for France and its representative. Stalin had no use for France, a onetime ally that, in the Soviet view, had capitulated to Germany virtually without a fight and, with the collaborationist Vichy government in power in the southern half of France, had submissively cooperated with the Germans—even though Stalin himself had been an ally of Hitler from 1939, until the German surprise invasion, Operation Barbarossa, started in June 1941. Stalin regarded France as a negligible quantity, and he did not conceal his contempt.

But Catroux had one great quality: he was a man of decision. He had the determination of a fox terrier—he never gave up. Once he had analyzed a question, he made a decision, and he didn't back down. He executed. Catroux was a career military man from a career military family. He met Charles de Gaulle in 1915 during World War I, when both were prisoners of the Germans. He was the governor-general of French Indochina when World War II war broke out, and after the surrender of France to the Germans in June 1940, which occurred after a mere six weeks of fighting, he refused to follow orders issued by Vichy. Instead, he became the highest-ranking French military official to join de Gaulle's Free French. He fought in the Syrian campaign with the British, and after the Allies had expelled the Germans from North Africa, he became the Free French governor in Algiers, then, following the liberation of Paris and the creation of a French provisional government under de Gaulle, he was appointed ambassador to the Soviet Union.

He arrived in January 1945 to unseasonably cold weather, even by the standards of a Moscow winter. It was minus 15 degrees centigrade inside the embassy and minus 40 outside. Catroux was welcomed by Roger Garreau, a career diplomat who, like Catroux, had thrown in his lot with de Gaulle and the Free French. As soon as the provisional government was installed in Paris, de Gaulle had dispatched him to Moscow as his representative. With Catroux as the new ambassador, the two men formed a kind of military-civilian cooperation. Garreau, with his tortoiseshell glasses and scholarly air, was a product of the striped-pants ranks of diplomacy; Catroux, by contrast, tempered into steel by the fire of the war, represented the man of action.

The main task for both men was to execute de Gaulle's order for the repatriation of their compatriots. The Red Cross, whose various national affiliates were already crisscrossing the war-torn countries, seemed best placed to fulfill this mission. It was an institution recognized by all belligerents, sufficiently identifiable to be able to travel in safety. But Catroux and Garreau also needed a person of their own, someone French above all, who would report to them. The person chosen for the job was Madeleine Pauliac, a young medical doctor who, as of November 1944, held the rank of doctor-lieutenant.

Why a woman? Why Madeleine?

I've often wondered why she was chosen for this difficult, if not impossible mission. True, as we've noted, she had proven herself in the resistance and in the battles for the Vosges and Alsace. She was cool under fire, brave, and perhaps above all, patriotic. But Catroux, like Garreau, knew perfectly well that women were particularly at risk in this part of Europe, which was still being fought over. War, of course, is mortally treacherous for men, but women faced their own danger. They were up against rough, battle-hardened soldiers who, in the violent, inherently amoral conditions of war, often regarded women as spoils, offering sexual rewards for their sacrifice.

We know that Madeleine met General de Gaulle, who personally issued her orders. Exactly what they said to each other remains a mystery, but de Gaulle clearly wanted to give more responsibilities to women. It was he who in October 1944 offered women the right to vote in France, and they did vote for the first time in French history in the municipal elections of April 1945. De Gaulle wanted to give women like Madeleine more of a role in the affairs of the country. Beyond the historical necessity, given that France lagged behind other European countries in giving women the right to vote, there was another compelling demographic reason, too. In World War I, 1.5 million soldiers had died, resulting in a 40 percent decrease in men compared to single women. In World War II, an additional two hundred thousand soldiers died, most of them male. France was facing a deficit in the male population, and women would have to take up the slack.

But perhaps also, de Gaulle, and Catroux with him, wanted Madeleine not only to promote women, or because of her proven courage, but also because, despite the special dangers faced by women, they had an advantage over men in the more delicate tasks of diplomacy. Women could appear more "neutral" than men in a region still raw from warfare, where armed men were as likely to settle disputes with gunfire as they were through polite negotiation. Already, the repatriation of prisoners had often turned into an arm-wrestling match between the Red Cross on the one side and local authorities on the other for whom the repatriation of foreign nationals was at best a minor priority, at worst an insult, an invasion, or an interference. Sometimes in this sense, de Gaulle and Catroux might have felt, female diplomacy would be more effective than male strength.

In any case, it was Catroux who, on De Gaulle's orders, put Madeleine in charge of the repatriation mission, and he and Garreau gave her detailed instructios after she'd completed the last stage of her journey to Warsaw. They explained that she'd have to operate in a completely destroyed environment with little or no resources, in a place where nothing was left standing, where people were trying to survive despite the chaos, a harsh, frightening world where women were all too often objects of predation; a world whose reconstruction had not yet begun; a world that had yet to recover from the brutal excesses of human folly.

Chapter 2

A FIELD OF RUINS

(April 7–29, 1945)

The sight of the Soviet capital must have taken Madeleine by surprise. And that's putting it mildly. Coming from Paris, a city miraculously spared by the war and still as beautiful as ever, she found herself in a freezing place, battered by wind and snow, traversed by silhouettes bundled in rags. The people had suffered a great deal and were still suffering, and spring in Moscow was still a long way off, if the polar climate was anything to go by. After the heat of the Mediterranean, the contrast was violent.

I remember vividly my own first visit to the Soviet capital. I was fifteen years old and had chosen to learn Russian as a second language. It was on my own initiative, I thought, or was it really chance, or an unconscious choice to get closer to my aunt? I left in the summer of 1962 to join a Komsomol camp, the youth camp of the Communist Party of the Soviet Union. I was the third child in a family with a tradition of adventure. My parents let me go to a country that didn't fit in at all with their convictions. My father, a lawyer at the Court of Appeals, had taken over the job of running the family cannery, the place of my childhood memories, so he was a "boss." Why did he let me travel to the USSR? Perhaps my mother had insisted, with the angel Madeleine sitting on her shoulder? It was twenty years after the end of the war, and I retain a vision of a harsh, cold metropolis. It's not the only time I've walked in my aunt's footsteps without really knowing it. In high school, not only had I chosen to study Russian as my foreign language, but I was also among twenty or so French students who went to the Soviet Union on

11

a trip organized by the Franco-Russian Friendship Committee, spending two weeks on the banks of the Dnieper River, not far from Kyiv, the capital of Ukraine (which was then part of the Soviet Union) with an elite group of young communist boys aged sixteen to twenty-four. We, the young French, were impressed by the technological advances of the Russians in the conquest of space and the exploits of Yuri Gagarin, who, a year earlier, had become the first man to make a flight into space. I remember the Russian boys showing photos of Parisian department stores like Printemps and Galeries Lafayette and asking why people were waiting in lines there, believing that it must be because of rationing. I explained to them that the photos must have been taken a few moments before the doors opened and that they were propaganda. The trip continued in Moscow, where every day there were visits to museums and universities, and I remember an evening at the Bolshoi Theater for a magnificent ballet. Life in Moscow for us was cheerful and light, far from the sinister atmosphere Madeleine had known in 1945.

In Madeleine's time, April 1945, the city, the object of one of the fiercest and bloodiest battles of the war, was battered and bruised, but triumphant. The Battle of Moscow, taking place in the last three months of 1941, was the first major Nazi defeat of the war, costing the Germans 250,000 to 400,000 dead, wounded, and missing (compared to a staggering one million losses for the Russians). It was, in short, the beginning of the end for Germany, though the war still had more than three years to go. When Madeleine arrived there, portraits of Marx, Lenin, and Stalin were everywhere, and Madeleine was struck by this display. France, too, had its hero, de Gaulle, but his picture wasn't posted on walls and billboards everywhere you looked. In Moscow, the purpose of the posters was clear. It was to remind the people of what they owed to their leaders—past and present—and especially to the "Man of Steel," Joseph Stalin himself. The chief quality of the country was its iron discipline, its blind obedience to orders. The lesson was clear: when it came to Stalin, it was best not to oppose. Paranoia was permanent and repression ruthless.

The French Embassy was housed in the Igoumnov House, formerly owned by a family of wealthy industrialists. Built in the purest traditional Russian style, it was nationalized by the Soviets and leased to France before the war. It was there that General Catroux explained to Madeleine the details of her mission. He knew it was going to be a tricky one, and that the occupiers, the Red Army, would do nothing to help the French repatriate French nationals.

A few days before Madeleine's arrival, Catroux had had a discussion with Vyacheslav Molotov, he of the immense forehead and handlebar mustache who was Stalin's Commissar for foreign affairs. Catroux asked him, as a matter of standard protocol, what support the Soviet government was going to give him to ensure the search for and repatriation of his many compatriots, prisoners, or deportees, whom the Red Army was going to liberate as they advanced through Poland and Germany. Molotov's reply left him fearing the worst. "Why are they so impatient to get back to France?" he asked, whether sincerely or sarcastically it was hard to tell. "Don't they understand that the Red Army, by freeing them from the clutches of the Nazis, has rendered them an invaluable service? How can their feelings toward the Soviet leadership be dampened? How, just a few days away from victory, can they allow themselves to be so oblivious to the facts?"

There may also have been another side to Molotov's striking lack of enthusiasm for the repatriation mission. The French prisoners were free labor for the Soviets. They were available to work in their camps like beasts of burden, helping to rebuild the country. After all, weren't they on the wrong side during the war? It didn't matter if they were forcibly conscripted or taken prisoner. They'd fought for the Germans, or, at least, worked for them. They were potential traitors. They deserved no mercy, no help. Foreigners were not the only ones to be treated in this way. Stalin's principled position was that any man who fell into enemy hands was suspect. He had undoubtedly betrayed his military and his patriotic duty, which was to fight to the death, and if taken prisoner, to escape. When Russian prisoners of war returned from the German camps, they weren't welcomed with a thankful embrace for their sacrifice; they were sent to Siberian camps. They went from the German camp at Sobibor to the Russian camp in Murmansk on the Arctic Sea. Some of these returning soldiers, especially those with Party responsibilities, were executed as traitors.

General Catroux explained all this to Madeleine. She must understand that she couldn't count on the help of the occupying power, and she even had to fear that it would put obstacles in her way. Not to mention that Russian soldiers had a very bad reputation for violence and sexual predation. It was not good to be a woman around them. They were suspected of exactions, rapes, and murders, but you also didn't want to offend the great ally. So, it would be up to her, Catroux told her, to find a way through, using tact and cunning, as well as courage, imagination, and daring, to find those whom the Red Army did not want to be found.

Still, even after all these explanations and warnings, Madeleine couldn't wait to leave for Warsaw, where her mission awaited. But it would take nearly three weeks after her arrival in Moscow for things to get organized. Three weeks to gather material—there was nothing in Warsaw—and wait for the military situation, specifically the progress of the Red Army in driving the Wermacht out of Poland and across the border into Germany, to be settled enough for the trip to take place.

But time passes slowly when all your thoughts are fixed on a goal that circumstances prevent you from pursuing. Madeleine had shown herself to be determined, courageous, and strong-willed. Now she had to bide her time in the small room in the frigid embassy that had been allocated to her. She'd taken only a few things with her on her journey, including two photographs that I found in the papers entrusted to me by my mother. One shows a scene at the gate of the family's Villeneuve estate. There's the whole entourage: Anne-Marie, her sister; Jacques Maynial, her brother-in-law, with his little round glasses; Jacqueline and Cyliane, two childhood friends, looking amused. My mother barely recognizes herself in this photo: the dark jacket, the floral dress, the rolled-up socks—is it really her? Happy days, lost to the past.

Then there's a photo of Roger Pauliac, her father. He's posing for an official document—a pleasant face, a half smile, a distant gaze. "A very devoted and very brave officer, mortally wounded on March 30, 1916, when he was giving words of encouragement to the men of his corps under very heavy shelling," reads the inscription. Madeleine's father always held a very special place in her heart. Of course, she and her older sister were told many times about all his feats of arms, and they were proud of him and his devotion to his country—or they were supposed to be proud of his sacrifice, of his greatness in battle. And yet, when you're a little girl, how can you not be bitter, how can you not secretly wish that this admirable death had never happened? Madeleine remembers the

Figure 2.1   Posing atop a fence on the family property in Villeneuve-sur-Lot, during what later seemed like a halcyon time of innocent joy. The author's parents, Jacques and Anne-Marie Maynial, are on the right, with two family friends next to them, and Madeleine on the left. When Madeleine was on her mission in devastated Poland, she would ask herself what happened to the smiling young woman in this photo.

intimate family ceremony, observed every March 30, of placing of flowers on Roger Pauliac's grave, and every November 11, in a cemetery full of families coming to honor their dead. In the end, the only lesson their father had time to teach them was that you have to sacrifice.

Madeleine has no portrait of her fiancé, Gilles Saint-Vincent. We know very little about him, mainly from brief allusions to him in letters exchanged between Madeleine and two members of the Blue Squadron. Evidently he was an engineer, a graduate of either L'Ecole Polytechnique or L'Ecole des Ponts et Chaussées, the School of Bridges and Roads, both among France's most elite institutions, both in Paris, where he and Madeleine probably met and courted. It's not clear that he'd ever met Madeleine's family, or why he was in the United States, or when he went there. What is clear is that Madeleine considered herself Gilles's fiancée and that they would be apart for an undetermined length of time. They were not the only couple whose private plans were disrupted by the war. But whenever Madeleine had a minute, her mind flew to him. Knowing that he was there, waiting for her as she was for him, gave her strength. This war must end, and then life would be possible. They would meet again; they would be happy. Madeleine held on to the hope of family life. Her sister was already a mother, and she herself had not ruled out becoming one. She just had to finish what she had to do. A matter of duty, and fulfilling her duty had occupied so much of her life.

Madeleine owed much of her determination to her grandmother, her father's mother, a woman of strong character. Ever since her husband's death, she had run the family business with an iron fist, the canning factory in Villeneuve-sur-Lot, which provided them all with a comfortable lifestyle. Roger, her son, was supposed to take up the torch, but the Great War claimed him, like so many others. He left behind his two daughters, on whom his grandmother placed all her love and hopes. Anne-Marie and Madeleine, pampered and encouraged to become free, strong women. You couldn't rely on a husband; you had to be able to stand on your own two feet, in case of need, in any situation. It was a philosophy of life that had always accompanied the two sisters, and one that my mother passed on to me. World War I pushed and forced so many women to take over the reins of their lives, and World War II would have a similar effect. Women like my aunt, who were already quite independent, took on their responsibilities and made their mark. They were prepared for it. My aunt's childhood and circumstances made it possible.

Just as Madeleine was being briefed on the scope of her mission, important news reached the French Embassy in Moscow: the Nazi concentration camp at Buchenwald in Germany had been liberated. The French Interests Committee, along with other organizations, had taken control of the camp. The vise continued to tighten on Germany. This was not Madeleine's direct concern, but it was an event that signaled the beginning of another mission, that of the women of the Blue Squadron, still far away to the west, but heading in her direction.

Chapter 3

ON THE JOB

(April 29–May 2, 1945)

Since leaving Moscow, nothing had worked. The locomotive was running out of coal; the wagons were falling apart; the track was sometimes hastily repaired; water was becoming scarce; there were no toilets on board; the bread was black and the heating nonexistent.

Madeleine left with a full ton of equipment, which two Frenchmen from the Moscow embassy—Nicolas Lazare, General Catroux's aide-de-camp, and his deputy, whom we know only as Huang—helped her load onto the train. Just as she was about to leave the embassy, news arrived that Édouard Herriot, the leftist former prime minister, imprisoned in Germany because of his opposition to the Vichy government, had been liberated with his wife by the Red Army and were arriving at the Moscow airfield. Madeleine's departure was chaotic: everyone was running in every direction, but she was unperturbed, even amused. She wasn't thinking of politics or Herriot, though he was a major figure in France at the time, a symbol of resistance to German oppression and to the collaborationist government in Vichy, France, and his arrival in Moscow was headline news. Madeleine was concentrating on getting her cargo, consisting of a ton of medication and medical equipment, which she'd gotten together with great difficulty, on board the train amid the chaotic circumstances of the departure, amidst hundreds of anxious people, who had also waited for weeks and months for this train to Warsaw and who were now also getting their baggage on board and looking for seats. It was an immense responsibility, made even more difficult because Madeleine was traveling without an escort, fearing at every moment that the shipment could be requisitioned by the Russians or stolen. According to the German news magazine *Der Speigel*, writing decades later, Madeleine was almost surely already under surveillance by the NKVD, the main Soviet intelligence agency (predecessor to the later KGB), which would keep tabs on her during her entire sojourn in Poland. Herriot might have arrived at the Moscow airport, but for Madeleine, her mission was the only thing that mattered to her.

The train creaked into motion at 7 p.m., still light enough for Madeleine to note the ugliness and monotony of the landscape, before night began to fall. They moved slowly through a monotonous countryside. Ruined stations, swallowed up by an infinite plain sinking into darkness, disappeared one by one. Villages could be made out, but there were no distinct edges, no hills, no heights to mark the horizon, which drowned in permanent grayness.

The next day, when she opened her eyes, the train had stopped at a station whose name, written in Cyrillic letters, was incomprehensible. She copied it: "MNUYRHUCK." Word arrived that the track had been sabotaged up ahead. "Polish traitors," the stationmaster told her. He meant "partisans," the anti-Soviet resistance. Madeleine reopened her notebook and wrote, "April 30, ramparts on a hill, a station that's nothing but a pile of junk. Track repairs will take at least two hours." She took the opportunity to stretch her legs. On the platform, things were improving; women were selling milk, eggs, and potato pancakes. Still, misery lurked; there was a stench of mold and despair. A meager sun momentarily warmed the mud. All along the streets, it was the same desolate sight. Soviet soldiers, in tight, drunken, dirty groups, sang and threw empty bottles, before unloading their weapons against the sky. Shelters dug out of the ground revealed military positions; half-buried tanks appeared to have been abandoned. Madeleine wandered a bit farther. In front of the church, beggars sat on the median and in the cemetery, stoking anemic fires and heating old tin cans. Women, with newborn babies in their arms, wrapped in rags, silently prayed.

As a doctor, Madeleine couldn't ignore the disastrous sanitary conditions of the population. Everyone was hungry, and deprivation had left its mark on their bodies. Misery was everywhere, worse than the privations suffered by Parisians. If you were hungry in occupied Paris, you could still find a minimum of sustenance. And for Madeleine, parcels from Villeneuve-sur-Lot regularly reached their destination.

Six days before, on April 24, Soviet troops had entered Berlin. The Red Army's vengeance—every German was considered guilty—was terrible. Nobody escaped it, not women, children, or old men. It was like the pitch fire that ravaged the earth in the Old Testament: everything was burned, destroyed, charred, reduced to ashes, the flames running through the dust, infinite. The twenty-seven million Soviet corpses caused by the war demanded vengeance, and the Russian soldiers, driven by a boundless hatred, set about carrying out the will of their dead. A storm of steel and blood descended on the Reich.

In January 1945, Georgy Zhukov, commander of the Red Army on the Polish front, future Soviet minister of defense, had issued an order: "Cursed be the land of murderers. We will take revenge for everything." The final directive from the Military Political Administration, on entering East Prussia, was even clearer: "On German soil, there is only one master, the Soviet soldier. He is the judge and executioner avenging the torments of fathers and mothers, for the destruction of towns and villages. Remember: this is the family of murderers and oppressors." Girls older than twelve were raped or killed. Every house was looted. In one village, the Red Cross witnessed unimaginable atrocities. The German women committed suicide; the men disappeared. In one East Prussian village near Königsberg, people learned from the veterinary clinic that a shipment of horse meat had arrived. The mayor installed by the Reds, Hermann Matzkowski, a staunch communist, was himself horrified at what happened next: "Of all the women who came looking for food, not one of them returned home intact. They were all raped. And some didn't come back at all. The only inhabitants who were fed were the women knocked up by Russian soldiers." Even Matzkowski's seventy-one-year-old mother was raped. Official reason, mentioned in Matzkowski's report: the "desire for retribution." The direct consequence, deplored by the Soviet authorities, was the unbridled spread of venereal diseases. "These abominable crimes have not been punished by the state. Women have been raped in front of their children. We cite the case of the soldier who gave chocolate to a child while his buddy bullied the mother, laughing. And, once his business was done, a bullet in the head. Major General Mikhail Ivanovich Bourtsev, who is the main political leader of the Red Army of Peasants and Workers—PURKA— was informed. He simply stated that most of the women allegedly raped complained that they had been raped on the floor, not on the bed."

In the distance, on the plain, Madeleine saw heavy smoke rising above a pyre. She was coming to understand that the scale of the catastrophe was every bit as horrifying in Poland as it was in eastern Germany, with the difference that Poland was innocent, a victim, not a perpetrator. The country was martyred four times: once with the arrival of Soviet troops in 1939, after Hitler and Stalin agreed to divide up the country; again with the advance of Nazi soldiers toward the USSR in 1941, when Hitler launched his surprise attack against his erstwhile ally, Stalin; again with the withdrawal of the Nazi armies in 1944; and a fourth time now with the assault of the Red Army as it ground its way to Germany. In July 1944, when the Majdanek camp near Lublin was liberated, thousands of leaflets were spread by air. "Soldiers of the Red Army! Kill the Germans! Kill all Germans! Kill them! Kill! Kill! Kill!" The figures were overwhelming: in January 1945, three million German civilians living on Polish territory began to flee the Soviet front line. And in the ensuing months, the number almost doubled.

The Poles fared no better. At the Yalta Conference in February 1945, Roosevelt, Churchill, and Stalin had agreed to the formation of a Provisional Polish government, made up in large part by the wartime government in exile in London, which was closely linked to the main anti-German resistance in Poland, the Home Army. But Stalin also gained acceptance in Moscow of the pro-communist Polish Workers Party as part of a Polish coalition, and in exchange, he promised that after the war, free and fair elections would be held to choose a permanent Polish government.

But Stalin never intended to keep that promise. The whole arrangement was a ruse, with the ultimate purpose of establishing a Soviet-dominated puppet government. An indication of his intentions came in early April, when sixteen non-communist Polish figures were invited to Moscow presumably to negotiate their participation in the postwar provisional government, their safety guaranteed by the Allies. The representatives included the president of the Council of National Unity, the secretary-general of the Polish Socialist Party, a delegate of the Polish government-in-exile, and General Leopold Okulicki, the last wartime commander of the underground, anti-Nazi Home Army. The sixteen men were arrested, tortured by the NKVD, and, after being held for several months, convicted of various crimes (including spying for the Nazis) and sentenced to varying terms in prison. Okulicki, for example, died in a Moscow prison in December 1946. Apart from a perfunctory protest by Churchill, the United States and Britain did nothing to stop the Russians, whose aim was to eliminate the leaders of all the independent Polish political groups.

Gradually, as Madeleine's train rumbled westward, the scene changed. The black ponds were covered with yellow buds. The birch trees were flowering. The snow disappeared. Storks fluttered and snapped their beaks on rooftops. Meadows turned green. The train arrived in Brest-Litovsk on what is now the Polish–Belarussian border, and Madeleine noted what she called "my first sight of a refugee train. There are around 6,000 Ukrainians there, men, women, children returning from Germany. Everyone is milling about, running everywhere, cooking their meals along the tracks; everything is smoking, and it smells bad." She saw women relieving themselves on the street, without privacy, but also without embarrassment. Time passed. The trains didn't move. There were Belgian, Dutch, Italian, and Hungarian wagons—and French ones, too. The population movements at the end of the war were tragic and frustrating. But the sight of these haggard men, women, and children with blank eyes was, in its way also awe-inspiring. *We absolutely have to help them*, Madeleine thinks, *to put this wounded and lost humanity back on its feet.*

"We wait for six hours," she wrote in her diary. "My papers are checked, and the train leaves for Poland. On the entire Russian route, I won't see a single intact station, not a single entire city." She'd been on the train for two days by then, stopping and starting. May 1 was spent amid an appalling smell of latrines, and May 2 was still drowned in the morning gloom. Finally at 6 a.m., the Russian ticket inspector opened the compartment door and announced: "Praga-Warzawa," and the train stopped as if exhausted from its effort. Warsaw-Praga!

Madeleine stepped onto the platform. The station—or whatever stood in for it—was deserted. No one was waiting for her. She walked to a ticket booth that she saw in the distance, and there addressed the attendant. Attendant of what? In any case, he was upset to be disturbed. She told him she'd like to call the French embassy.

Niet telefon!

She searched her memory for the Russian word that meant "Where?" *Gdié?*

The man threw up his hands; there was no phone or electricity. He mimed lighting a cigarette: "*Tabak?*" No, she didn't have tobacco for this useless lout. She would later note in her notebook, "He told me to go to hell."

Outside, slabs of ice were melting. Where was the embassy? Roger Garreau, who'd left Moscow for Warsaw before her, must already be there. Decidedly, the "Western bloc" was a sorry sight in the zone "liberated" by the Soviets. She wants to lash out, but she's been warned in Moscow: under article 58 of the Soviet code, the slightest criticism of the regime or the state immediately earned the author a stay in the Far North. There were prying ears ready to hear the slightest inappropriate word. An army of informers worked day and night, in the interests of the dictatorship of the proletariat. Stalin explained it well: Soviet citizens enjoyed full freedom—within certain limits.

Madeleine could only rely on herself, but that didn't scare her. She got help, unloaded her crates and bags, and found a cart on which to pile them. The cart moved off, and Madeleine, "perched on her parcels" made her way through the streets of Warsaw's Praga district toward what served as her embassy.

When I read this passage from her notes, I confess I felt great admiration for my aunt, but I also shuddered at the thought of Madeleine arriving in this devastated city. All the descriptions of Warsaw at this time are like Dante's Inferno. Imagine my aunt, a young woman of thirty-two, arriving alone in this shattered, martyred place, where she spoke not a word of the language, managing the unloading of a ton of sacks and crates, using sign language to find someone to get her a cart and to load it up, and then somehow managing to find her destination.

Her first sight was of the cross on the steeple of the Orthodox church, hanging pitifully over its side. "The weather is gray," she wrote. "I look at ruined houses, piles of ruins; a wrecked church in the distance is a sinister vision of a Warsaw that has been dismantled, devastated, the church's two towers dominating a vision of catastrophe." It was about a mile and a half from the Praga Poludnie station, the terminus for trains coming from the East, to the French embassy. A graphic novel based on Madeleine's life, due to be published in France in 2025. shows her walking alongside a horse-drawn carriage with her shipment on top of it. We're not sure this is accurate; in any case, she got to the embassy somehow, probably wondering why neither Garreau nor anybody else came to the station to meet her. But it's an emblem of the general disorder. Nobody in the embassy could have known when her train would arrive, given that it had left three days earlier and had made numerous lengthy stops along the way, adhering to no knowable schedule. The embassy itself was on the second floor of a gray, dirty house in Warsaw's eastern district. The prewar embassy was in the elegant Frascati Palace in the center of Warsaw, but when official French representatives were able to return to Poland in 1945, they had rented this private house in the near suburbs. Other embassies, including the American, were in the Polonia Hotel, all of them waiting for a semblance of normalcy before seeking permanent quarters. The French quarters at least had the advantage of being across the street from what soon became the French Hospital, created by Madeleine.

Madeleine had reached the goal of her journey. Her mission could begin.

Chapter 4

FRANCE IN POLAND
(May 2–Early June, 1945)

To be reunited with her compatriots after days spent on the train, alone, amid the chaos, surrounded by a polyglot crowd, unable to exchange more than a few words, was a joy Madeleine had not anticipated. Everyone here had a particular background. There was Roger Garreau, whom she already knew, the diplomat who came from Moscow to establish French representation in this devastated city and lead negotiations for the repatriation of French prisoners. He was, as one of his colleagues put it, "inventive and non-conformist." Madeleine also met Francis Huré and Christian Fouchet, the diplomats whom de Gaulle had sent to forge ties with the Poles, including the Polish communists in Lublin, in the hopes of getting their cooperation in the repatriation mission. Fouchet was a former pilot who had originally gone to Moscow as part of a Free French military mission known as the Normandy Regiment, and he appears to have been the first Westerner to get to liberated Warsaw, traveling there with the Red Army. A colleague described him as a large and imposing man who "in the crazy confusion of events and men . . . represented a force that moved." He'd established excellent contacts with the communists and even had a source among the pro-Moscow Poles in Lublin, who were competing for influence with the non-communist Polish government-in-exile in London.

This is key to understanding the political background to the entire French repatriation effort in Poland. During the various Allied summit meetings that took place during the war, in Teheran, Yalta, and, shortly after the German surrender, at Potsdam, Roosevelt, Stalin, and Churchill

25

agreed in principle that there would be free elections in Poland, leading to what President Roosevelt liked to call "a strong, independent, and prosperous nation, with a government ultimately to be selected by the Polish people themselves." Technically, Stalin's promotion of the Lublin Committee was simply a gesture aimed at broadening the existing provisional Polish government, making it more representative and democratic. In fact, the committee, made up mostly of hardened communists who'd spent the war in Moscow and were loyal to Stalin, was the Trojan horse by which the communists would undermine any chance for a real Polish democracy to emerge in the ruins of the war.

Fouchet, well-informed about Stalin's intentions, would have conveyed to the French delegation in Warsaw what the Russian goals were in connection with Madeleine's activities in Poland. They would tolerate the French repatriation mission operating on Polish soil, but they had imposed a diplomatic precondition: recognition of the communist government favorable to Moscow against the one in exile in London, or there would be no cooperation. And because France, as a member of the western alliance, was duty-bound to recognize the London government-in-exile, the communists' condition spelled considerable trouble for Madeleine's mission ahead. "Nothing in Lublin could be decided without the agreement of Moscow," Huré later wrote.

Reading Madeleine's notes, I was struck by the simplicity of the relationship between these men and women in the newly reopened French embassy. You can feel the open camaraderie, the desire to build and work together, with no personal ambitions or ulterior motives. Later, when they arrived, the young women of the Blue Squadron would also feel this camaraderie. Was this due only to the fact of distance, to their being so far from home? I don't think so. There must have been an element of humility in those who, having been defeated, nevertheless continued the fight, first in isolation, then in ever-increasing numbers. One senses in all these men and women who had resisted the occupation at home (and not in those who joined the movement after victory) a desire to change the world, to improve society, to engage in some self-sacrifice that might be due to religious convictions, but wasn't necessarily.

Jacqueline Saint-Guily is one who found shelter among the compatriots at the embassy. She was very moved to see someone arriving from her homeland, a representative of Free France, who could bring news from home and remind her what normal life was like. Jacqueline had lived a thousand lives. Her father received thirteen commendations during the Battle of Verdun in the First Great War (World War I). Her first husband, a naval captain, was killed in the early days of the second; in fact, she was the first war widow of 1939. He was in command of a minesweeper, the *Pluton*, she explains. He was sent to lay mines in Casablanca, opposite the port. There was an explosion, then a chain reaction, and everyone died—two hundred sailors. Debris was found two kilometers away. After that, she married Lieutenant-Commander Paul Saint-Guily, with whom she joined the Resistance. But she was denounced, arrested, and interned at Fresnes, just south of Paris, and then deported to Ravensbrück, the women's camp in the north of Germany, where, at its height, some 132,000 women were detained, many of them in forced labor. Jacqueline was liberated from there by the Red Army, after which she made her way to Warsaw. She asked Madeleine a thousand questions, questions that almost all French people long estranged from their homeland were asking.

Was it true that the Eiffel Tower had been destroyed?

Madeleine reassured her. That particular unfounded rumor had spread widely among French prisoners and deportees.

Jacqueline Saint-Guily was determined to stay and help her compatriots who had managed to reach this tiny piece of France amid the ruins. The woman doctor who had just arrived, with her sporty appearance and warm gaze, encouraged her all the more.

Charles Liber, a doctor, had been forced by the Germans to work in a camp in Poland, and when he was liberated by the Russians, he elected to postpone his departure for home, even though he'd been away a long time. He was a tall, lean man, smiling despite his serious appearance, and something sweet emanated from him. The side parting of his hair, the tortoiseshell glasses, the big nose, and that particular way he buried his head in his shoulders, as if he were waiting for a storm to pass. The Liber family had been doctors from father to son for at least three generations, in Walincourt, in the north of France. Charles, one of thirteen siblings, followed in their footsteps. He graduated from medical school in 1932, was mobilized in 1939 with the rank of doctor-lieutenant (the same as Madeleine), and was taken prisoner by the Germans the same year. He ended up in Hohenstein-Ernstthal in Saxony, where he set up the hospital's surgical department, then became head of the tuberculosis ward.

It was in this position that he began to help his countrymen, French prisoners being treated there, making sure that those who were in the worst shape stayed longer than necessary in his ward so they could fully regain their strength. Two years later, in 1944, when the Nazis discovered his stratagem, Liber was sent to Oflag IIB in Poland, a camp reserved for officers who refused to collaborate. In January 1945, the Germans evacuated the camp, leaving Dr. Liber and two colleagues to care for the wounded who could not be moved. When the Red Army arrived, it ordered him to stay, but he escaped, and he had been in Warsaw since March 1945. He had been asked to stay by the Polish Red Cross, but then he voluntarily decided to continue his work there. Despite his impatience to be reunited with his family, who had been struggling for years to have him released, he, too, felt the need to remain. The oath he took when he'd become a doctor held him there, an oath that was his foundation in the turmoil of war.

In the course of my research, I met Dr Liber's son, Benoît Liber, also a doctor, who had taken over the family practice in Walincourt. I found him in the phone book on the off chance there would still be a Dr. Liber there and gave him a call. He told me about a trip he and his two brothers had taken as teenagers to Poland with their father, Charles, who'd died in 1993 at the age of ninety-three. Charles Liber, who had never talked about the war with his sons, took them to Warsaw. There, they met a woman who had been a nurse at the French Hospital, but they were forbidden to ask her a single question—not a word. Their father never explained anything to them, never told them anything. When I told the young Dr. Liber about the research I had undertaken to learn about my aunt, and what I knew about his father, he broke down in sobs, learning for the first time what Charles Liber had done during the war but had kept secret. Why? Because he didn't want to experience anew his suffering? Because he wanted to spare his sons the knowledge of it? The silence of parents is often an invitation to seek the truth.

At the embassy, Madeleine also met Major Jean Neurohr, who'd also come from Moscow, assigned to the military mission to repatriate the French. After the German invasion, he'd joined General de Gaulle in

London and was in charge of the BBC's Alsatian broadcasts from August 1942 to September 1943, when he left for Algiers, newly liberated by the Allies with help from the Free French. The forced conscription of French citizens by the Germans was a crucial issue for him, one he spoke of regularly in his broadcasts. In May 1944, he left Algiers for Moscow and then went to Poland in early 1945, bent on helping the conscripted men who were still unable to return to France.

In all, when the French Mission of Repatriation in Poland was officially created, there were some twenty volunteers, most of them, like Dr. Liber, having been freed from prisoner-of-war camps. Madeleine and Charles Liber were the only two medical doctors in the group. The military commander of the mission was a Colonel Poix, about whom little is known, not even his first name, except that, like many of the others, he'd served time in a German prisoner-of-war camp liberated by the Soviets.

In December 1944, with de Gaulle heading the provisional French government in Paris and the German army expelled from France, the Russians and the French signed a preliminary agreement providing for all French prisoners of war to be sent back to France. Because fighting was still going on in Central Europe, at first most of them returned to France via ship from the Black Sea port of Odessa to Marseille. The first boat arrived in Marseille on April 15, and there were several other arrivals later. From June 29 to July 1, 1954, de Gaulle himself went to Moscow, and further agreements dated June 29 were signed, including one that concerned the return of French prisoners of war who had been captured wearing German uniforms.

But there were seemingly insuperable barriers faced by the French team when it came to actually implementing the agreements. Many men were suffering from injuries too serious to make the long trip by train to Odessa and then by boat to Marseille. Even before Madeleine arrived, many of these men had been rounded up by the Russians and brought to a camp, known as Rambertow, about five miles from Warsaw, where there was a Polish Red Cross dispensary. Between one hundred and five hundred men managed to get there every day, but because of the devastation of Poland, supplies, even as basic as bandages, were in very short supply, and the treatment was basic, at best. In the absence of bandages, wounds were wrapped in newspaper. There was no anesthetic for operations. The men were also hungry, but there wasn't much food to give them, clean drinking water was in short supply, and the electricity didn't work.

And that's why, when Madeleine arrived with an entire ton of medicine and clothing from Moscow, there was an explosion of joy among the members of the French team. The supplies meant life itself for the wounded prisoners.

Once first aid was administered, the men left, if they could, for places designed for evacuation. Prisoners knew there were boats to Marseille leaving from Odessa, and even though the trip there was exhausting, they headed for the port using every means of transport available. But others, too badly off, waited, hoping the road to Berlin would soon open and that a corridor from there to France would become passable. Others didn't go to Odessa because of rumors, apparently false, that the ships leaving from there were unseaworthy and sometimes sank.

For those who were too ill to travel, Roger Garreau had arranged a hospital ward for them at the dispensary, and there, under Madeleine's guidance, a triage center was set up. Garreau used his position as delegate of the Provisional Government of the French Republic to obtain some paint, and volunteers freshened up and repaired the walls, which had been damaged by the war. The president of the Polish Red Cross, Ludvig Christians, had fourteen beds and mats delivered, and they were installed. Word of the establishment of this health center got around, and local Poles began arriving, in the hope of getting treatment.

At the same time, Madeleine was learning how to undertake the treasure hunt involved in finding her compatriots. It was a matter of gleaning information from whatever source was available and following up on it. Fouchet introduced her to an informant that he had; then he was assigned to a new post in India, leaving Madeleine and the informant to maintain direct contact, and in that way she learned where some French citizens were being held, often in hospitals or detention camps. Some prisoners who made their way to the Red Cross clinic told her what they'd seen or what they'd been told, creating a web of rumors mixed with some accurate information. Another key member of the repatriation mission was Paul Ducroquet, a French officer with the designation of squadron commander, who had escaped with Liber in

January 1945 from Oflag IIB. They made their way to Warsaw, where, looking for a French official, they found Roger Garreau. He asked them to help set up the repatriation reception center and incorporated them into the staff of the fledgling embassy. Since his arrival, Ducroquet had set up intelligence networks to find Frenchmen held by the Russians. Together with Madeleine, they organized missions to recover these lost men. Ducroquet often accompanied Madeleine, and later, the nurses and ambulance drivers of the Blue Squadron, mainly in an effort to ensure their safety.

Their first outing, which was to be followed by many others, was marked by exaltation and hope, as well as a sort of joyful bravado that echoed in the journal of Simone Saint-Olive, one of the Blue Squadron members who arrived later. The task required courage and a certain amount of recklessness. Madeleine managed to obtain an ambulance and some petrol from the Polish Red Cross. She rode shotgun while Liber drove, negotiating a road that was hardly a road at all. The wheels spun, got stuck; they got out and pushed, and the vehicle set off again, bumpily overtaking platoons of Russian soldiers heading east, riding jeeps and pushing carts loaded with loot of all sorts—cupboards, sideboards, forks, bicycles. Patriotic songs were heard, and sometimes gunshots; it was a Soviet truck asking to pass. Sometimes, when they needed a push, the Ivans, as they called the Red Army troops, lent a hand.

But more often, the looks the French team got were envious, suspicious. Foreigners were obviously prime prey for theft or worse, especially if the foreigner was a woman. All along the road there was no color at all. It was all gray. Where were the Poles? Had they all been shot? A red and white flag, sometimes planted on a church, displayed the eagle, the Polish coat of arms. German signs, in Gothic letters, pointed to a village or locality. Everything seemed abandoned. The fields were empty, and so was the sky. Fifty kilometers from Warsaw, at last, a sign in French: "Camp Madelon." It's here, in what passed for a clinic, that a few French officers had gotten care, or so they'd been told. The ambulance passed through a market where nothing but cabbages were sold. In front of a low building, it stopped.

"We're going to try to find our people," Madeleine said, a look of determination on her face.

She was the first to go inside. Were they among the victors of the war? Nothing indicated that. A man in a dirty white coat stepped forward.

"French people? Are there any French people?" she asks.

Niet.

The man, a Russian, didn't speak French. Madeleine stepped toward him and tried German. The exchange was more fruitful. It wasn't that the man was hostile; it was just that he had his orders. No, no, there were no Frenchmen. She took Liber aside, said something to him. She returned to the Russian, pulled a pack of Lucky Strikes from her pocket, held out a cigarette, and she tried out her limited Russian when he looked at it.

"*Niet frantsous? Pravda?*" No French? True?

The man in the white coat looked left and right, took a cigarette, his face lit up.

"*Zwei.*" Two.

She handed the pack of Lucky Strikes to the man. He looked at her intently, from head to toe, and after two delicious puffs of Virginia tobacco, added, mixing German and Russian:

"*Fünf. Bistro, bistro.*" Five. Quickly, quickly.

A few minutes later, the first five French members of the recovery mission were settled, as best they could be, in the ambulance. Two of them were suffering from tuberculosis; the others were terribly emaciated.

The ambulance sped off, and at the first bend, out of sight of the miserable clinic, everyone sang: "*C'est une fleur de Paris, Du vieux/ Paris qui sourit, car c'est la fleur du retour.*" (It's a flower from Paris, Old Paris/ which smiles. Because it's the flower of returning.)

Mission accomplished, but just one. De Gaulle had spoken of five hundred thousand Frenchmen behind the Oder-Neisse line. Many had taken the road alone to Odessa, but how many were still waiting, in hospitals or Soviet prison camps?

Hitler committed suicide two days before Madeleine Pauliac arrived in Warsaw. The war was over. In a few days, the armistice would be signed. But in this devastated land, all was not yet over. France's lost soldiers must be found. Time was running out. This first mission "outside the walls" gave them energy. Save the men by going out to find them, one by one if need be; they would do it! But they needed reinforcements.

Chapter 5

STAYING ON YOUR FEET

(June 1945)

Photographs of Poland haunt me, Poland crushed, massacred, burned and charred. And, unfortunately, there are so many echoes of these photos in the history of our own times. The horror repeats itself over and over. We do not seem to be able to stop it.

In the past few days, Madeleine had come to realize the full extent of the devastation—the imprint of Nazism, Prussian cruelty, Soviet fury, chaos. One people tried to extinguish another. How could this country ever be reborn? And yet, despondency did not prevail. Was it because there was so much to do that she asked no questions and just worked relentlessly? Did the sheer scale of the task drown any inclination to give up? Every action was another step forward. Everything counted.

In the streets, the war was still on everyone's mind. Madeleine met people who looked away, lowered their heads, as if the terror were still present. The Warsaw uprising, organized by the Armija Krajova, the Polish Home Army, the AK, the main resistance group in the country, loyal to the government in exile in London, took place between August and October 1944. The Poles fought like tigers against the Nazis, and with the Red Army approaching Warsaw, they were encouraged by the Soviets to take decisive action. The Russians, having crossed the Pripet marshes, arrived in their tanks on the other side of Warsaw's Vistula River, prompting the Poles to believe, in a burst of hope, that their rescue was near. They erected barricades and began an uprising against the Nazi occupiers seeking to drive them out. The Russians, they believed, would support them.

But the Russians did nothing. Stalin was already determined to crush the Polish forces, whose allegiance was to the London government, but now he was able to advance that goal by sitting still as the Germans did the job for him. For twenty days, the Red Army watched through binoculars on the other side of the river as the Germans crushed the uprising and then took revenge for it—street by street, house by house, they destroyed the city, methodically, using dynamite and flame-throwers. Stalin himself gave the order not to cross the river. Hitler let loose the dogs.

Warsaw burned for three months, so that when the Ivans finally did cross the river, they "liberated" a city of corpses and rubble. As if that wasn't enough, the "Organes," the NKVD, finished the job, shooting Polish survivors.

Madeleine listened to the story of these days at the embassy. Her mission concerned the French, and yet—and yet, it was hard not to see the prevailing misery, the street children wandering around in search of a little food, and since they could always find some at the dispensary, she saw them there, ragged and thin.

The sight of children often brought her back to her own childhood, on the banks of another river far away in time and circumstance. She was marked by the death of her father, the hero she hardly knew, a tutelary shadow who, though absent, accompanied her and her sister in the construction of their personalities. Madeleine was pampered by her grandmother, a strong woman who took over the reins of the family cannery after the death of her only son. Their mother, Arsène Pauliac, née Coggia, suggesting Corsican origins, left Villeneuve-sur-Lot as soon as she was widowed. She moved to Nice with her two daughters, a city that Madeleine and her sister grew to loathe. Arsène was at odds with many people, including her mother-in-law, to the point that she refused to allow her the right to see her granddaughters. The case was settled in court, a first for that epoque, which put them in an uncomfortable position, torn between their mother and their grandmother. From then on, Madeleine and Anne-Marie spent their vacations entirely with their grandmother, and they were spoiled, playing tennis, horseback riding, and skiing.

When they got their high school diplomas, they decided to move to Paris together—"free at last!" they exclaimed—where their grandmother housed them with dignity and gave them an allowance so they could study and live independently. Their grandmother didn't refuse them a thing. As her heirs, they also benefited from her advice: be independent; never depend on a man—that was what she instilled in them. Madeleine and Anne-Marie were brought up, in part, by a feminist of the first instance—from that generation of women who, from the very first days of World War I, had to face the absence of their husbands, the fathers of their children, and, in the case of tens of thousands of them, permanently.

The only male figure in the sisters' lives during this period was their uncle, Antoine Coggia, who was a prefect of the Pyrénées-Atlantiques department, a member of the Radical-Socialist Party, who came to the aid of his sister, Arsène Pauliac, supporting her as well as her two girls. From him, they learned devotion to government service, as well as the bonds of a Corsican family and clan. Despite the misfortune of losing their father, a wind of optimism blew through their youth, and my mother used to tell me about their carefree times. The sisters went on expeditions to the mountains; they canoed down the Dordogne or the Lot, feeling free. There are 9.5 millimeter Pathé Baby home films shot by Madeleine and my mother that bring me back to the past. Graceful silhouettes in black and white, the two girls bathed in the rivers, pitched tents on their banks, and bivouaced in the wilderness. It was an idyllic moment. World War I was terrible, but it was now over, and there was a sense of rekindled faith in a better future.

What a contrast to the lives of the poor Polish orphans whom Madeleine was now seeing in the ruins of Warsaw. Times were hard for adults, but they were even worse for children. After medical school, Madeleine, as we've noted, performed tracheostomies at the Hospital for Sick Children in Paris. This was not an easy procedure. It had to be performed with perfect precision in emergency situations, at the risk of causing permanent damage to the larynx or vocal cords. When faced with an obstruction of the airway, the doctor must quickly incise the bottom of the child's trachea, just in the hollow formed by the junction of the clavicles, to allow the insertion of a tube for the passage of air. There was no allowance for the hand to tremble. Madeleine proved she had the necessary composure, which she was going to need here in Poland in every way.

Figure 5.1   Madeleine on skis reminds me of an entire epoque that I couldn't have known about as a child. Today, after the passage of so many years, I see in this image a happy face and a happy time.

The information the find-and-repatriate team received through various channels led them down sometimes-difficult paths. For example, they learned of the presence of a French contingent in Katowice, about three hundred miles southwest of Warsaw near the Czech border. But it was a group from the French militia, commanded by the fascist leader Joseph Darnand, the right-wing officer in the French army, a hero of World War I, who threw in his lot with the collaborationist Vichy government, organizing the *milice*, the much-feared, pro-fascist paramilitary police force that tracked down Jews and turned them over to the SS, as well as members of the anti-fascist, anti-Vichy resistance. Darnand had gone so far as to pledge an oath of loyalty to Hitler and had become an officer in the Waffen SS. After the Allied landing in Normandy, he fled to Germany along with some of the members of the *milice*, who volunteered to continue the fight on behalf of the Germans. As the Allies were closing in, Darnand escaped to Italy (where he was arrested later by the British and sent back to France, where he was put on trial and executed as a traitor). But with their leader gone and on the run, some of the soldiers under his command tried to insinuate themselves into French groups slated for repatriation.

These Waffen SS volunteers presented a delicate problem. What should be done? Abandon them or repatriate them? They could, of course, be brought to trial for their "acts of collaboration" once they returned to France. These were men who had just spent the war as guards in internment camps, where they gave help to executioners. But was the matter of their treatment now for doctors to decide, or the police? In any case, most of them didn't give their real names, hoping that by confusing matters, their pasts could be forgotten, and they would be able to start from zero.

Madeleine Pauliac and Charles Liber nevertheless left for Katowice. They had both taken an oath, the Hippocratic Oath, which stated in part, "I will respect all people, their autonomy and their will, without any discrimination according to their condition or beliefs."

We need to save and heal.

After ten days in the ambulance, Madeleine and Liber arrived at a camp a few kilometers from Katowice. She immediately spotted the feldgrau uniforms of the German army that the men were wearing, and she exchanged glances with Liber. You had to control yourself, to see only the men and not the uniforms. However, there was another problem. They suspected some Germans were among these prisoners, trying to escape the Russians by claiming that they were from Alsace or Lorraine, the regions of France west of the Rhine, where the local dialect was similar to that spoken in German east of the river. To confound this effort, Colonel Poix, head of the military mission, relied on French officers from Alsace and Lorraine, who were able to tell from the men's accents, which side of the Rhine any given prisoners were from.

One of the guys approached. He was French.

"So, what's the news in Alsace?" He smiled.

Liber replied: Alsace burned, but it was liberated. The French tricolor was flying over Strasbourg Cathedral.

"And Darnand?"

"He's on the run."

Madeleine asked the man a few questions: How many French were there? Answer: two hundred. Who controlled the camp? The Soviets. What did they intend to do? Send the prisoners east. To do what? God only knew. Were there any sick people? Yes, of course there were. Could they load them up? No, the Russians (who regarded the miliciens— members of the paramilitary French groups that collaborated with Nazi Germany—as traitors subject to execution) wouldn't allow that.

And so, the ambulance returned empty to Warsaw, with Madeleine swearing to herself that she'd never be in that situation again. From then on, she'd fight, if need be.

But the complications were endless. Not only were there French nationals in the camps who fought on the German side, but there were also Poles who fought in France as part of the Resistance. Poles fought in the Gard and Isère regions; the Kosciuszko battalion bore arms in the Loire; the Mickiewicz battalion cut the Nazis to shreds in Grenoble. Some of these men were now in Soviet-controlled camps, and they went to be freed to go to Warsaw. Before he left for India, Fouchet conducted complicated negotiations with the Soviets regarding these men. The Soviets wanted to know more about them, which of the Poles who fought for the Resistance in France were communists and which were not.

Poles wishing to return to Warsaw had to be identified by the Soviets, who wanted to sort out "ours" from the others. It was all part of the relentless Soviet program to weaken the non-communist

Figure 5.2   Dr. Charles Liber, who went to Warsaw straight from a camp where he was held a prisoner of war by the Germans. He and Madeleine operated as a team in setting up the French Hospital and crisscrossing Poland in search of French citizens in need of help.

alternative in Poland and to pave the way for a puppet communist regime. To that end, in July 1944, Stalin installed the Polish Committee of National Liberation in the city of Lublin, a group of pro-communist Poles who had spent the war until then in Moscow. Eventually, the Lublin Committee, recognized by Moscow, would take power from the non-communist government in exile in London, recognized by the West. It was the Lublin Committee, helped by the Red Army, that was in charge in some of the camps, and it wanted to take a census of the liberated French, to determine, presumably, which among them had fought on the German side and therefore should not be repatriated. The problem was that France did not recognize the Lublin authorities, whose very existence as Stalin's Polish cat's paw was contrary to the

Yalta agreement. The legitimate government was the one in London, in exile. But who could fight against the USSR, whose troops in Poland occupied the territory?

Back in Warsaw once again, Madeleine and Liber learned that they had been given a separate building for their work. It was a stone building just across the street from the embassy, and Roger Garreau, using his personal funds, fit it out as the "French Hospital." A streetcar passed in the distance, the first to be put back into service. Life seemed to be returning to normal.

When I went to Warsaw in 2016, there for the debut of the film *Les Innocentes*, I set out in my spare time to find the French Hospital, though I imagined that everything had been destroyed and that a modern building would occupy the site in a city that had essentially been rebuilt from scratch after its wholesale destruction. Nothing from the immediate postwar period could still exist, I thought. But after a lot of searching and dashed hopes, I found the building intact. It was empty. I posed for a photo in front of the staircase, located at Kryniczna 6. It's a curved street, now surrounded by greenery. The building hasn't changed, except for a glass roof installed along the terrace. The color of the stones is still the same, a kind of bland beige that weathering hasn't altered. The top of the railing has been painted brown, as has the base of the staircase—all intact. After about 1960, the Tunisian Embassy occupied the premises, which are now offices.

When I visited, a sign announced, "For rent."

Jacqueline Saint-Guily was the first to leave, along with Francois Huré, who had arrived in Moscow in 1943 and, with Fouchet, was the first to take charge of the issue of French prisoners in the Soviet zone. Huré's departure would remove from the scene one of the best-informed of the French officials in Warsaw. And not only was he leaving, the much-loved Dr. Liber was also returning to France. Liber would be universally missed, but at last, after the long years of the war and his volunteer service in Poland, he would be reunited with his family and friends in France, which he hadn't seen in five years, just as the French Hospital he so earnestly hoped for opened its doors. The little group, tightly knit in the mud and ruins of Warsaw, was scattering.

Figure 5.3   Madeleine alongside Philippe Garreau, the son of Roger Garreau, who was effectively France's ambassador to Poland and who, during the difficult months of Madeleine's mission, did everything he could to help her.

But amid the sadness of these departures, Garreau reported some good news: a group of French nurses and ambulance drivers was coming to Warsaw to lend a hand with the troubled repatriation effort. They would be under the command of Lieutenant Pauliac. Garreau didn't know exactly when these newcomers would arrive, but the mere prospect of receiving reinforcements boosted everyone's morale.

Chapter 6

THE BLUE SQUADRON

(April 25, 1945)

Just as Madeleine arrived in Moscow and was awaiting her departure for Warsaw, Simone Saint-Olive, known as "Sainto," was discovering Paris. I had the good fortune of meeting her as I did my research on Madeleine and got her firsthand stories. She was twenty-four years old in 1945, a nurse at the Desgenettes Military Hospital in Lyon, also a leader in the Guides de France, the country's equivalent of the Girl Scouts, and she was deeply influenced by the values the organization promoted, including a spirit of solidarity and helping one another. Now, with Paris liberated and the Allies, led by the United States, marching into Germany, she had joined the French Red Cross. In Paris, she marveled at everything: the metro, the grand buildings and museums, and also the magnificent Austin ambulances that had been donated to the French Red Cross by the king of England. At the movies one night, she saw the newly released *Les Enfants du Paradis, Children of Paradise*, directed by Marcel Carné, the great love story set in the theatrical world of Paris in 1830, starring Jean-Louis Barrault, and she was transported by it. After a few days, she was assigned to Red Cross Mobile Group 1, headed by Violette Guillot. Her ambulance partner was Jeanine Robert, aka Petit Bob. Among the others in the group was Micheline Reveron, known as "Miche," another nurse with a personal motivation to do her part: her fiancé had been killed in Alsace at the start of the war. There were eleven in all, six nurses, five drivers, including Charlotte Pagès, Jacqueline Heiniger, Aline Tschupp, Cécile Stiffler, Elisabeth Blaise, Simone Braye, and Francoise Lagrange.

Together, they set off to the east in their robust, but bulky, boxy vehicles, five of them, for Metz, then Saint-Avold, approaching the German border, following in the wake of the American army. Sainto described in her notebook the ravaged France they traverse: "Truncated trees, bloated horses, infinitely sad gray earth." The squadron sang the Marseillaise when they crossed the Rhine, but they kept driving even as night fell, until they arrived somewhere near Frankfurt. It was dark, and everyone was going to bed on pallets spread out inside the ambulances, but unwittingly, they'd stopped near an encampment of American GIs, who, all night long, tried to establish a "dialogue" with them.

"At one o'clock in the morning, all hell broke loose," Sainto recalled. "Half in English, half in French, they wanted Micheline and Pagès to open the doors for them. 'Open please. How many *Françaises*? *Coucher avec you* . . . ' They kept it up for a quarter of an hour, and it was unnerving. Micheline said, 'I'd rather be bombed.'" Finally, with the ambulances locked from the inside, the soldiers left, and the women in Sainto's ambulance called out to the women in the ambulance next to theirs. "Hello, Petit Bob!" Petit Bob was sleeping soundly despite the noise, but Sainto called out loudly enough to wake her up. "Do you hear?" Petit Bob replied, "Yes, everything's fine," and, exhausted from the long drive, went back to sleep. "In the end, I wake her up, because Micheline is wondering what she should do if she's attacked. Then we hear drums, trumpets. They're coming back! So Petit Bob gets dressed, and then, when the soldiers don't come back, she goes back to sleep. During this tragic-comic event, the women in the ambulance dressed and undressed five timed. It's our first night in Germany, after Alsace."

The next day, they were in Weimar, already well in the German east. There, on the airfield, the nurses made contact with a group of French prisoners, who stormed the ambulances and carried the women on their shoulders in triumph. The boys cried, swore, sang, and talked. They gave the women "hope and smiles," as Sainto put it. After a while, the ambulances left, and when an engine broke, Miche and Pagès repaired it, their hands in the grease. On April 25, they were in Gmund, in the snow and the cold. Along the way, they tended to the wounded. A deportee, who had stayed behind to help his comrades who were too sick or injured to leave on an earlier convoy, gave them a message to be delivered back home: "Tell my wife I'm all right."

Others said nothing and would never speak again, and the women's hearts hardened in anger in the midst of so much suffering. They came across empty hospitals, people dying en route, survivors lost forever. There was typhus, diarrhea, dirt, screams, complaints, sores, and corpses. In her diary, Sainto wrote, "I can't describe what I see, I have hatred in my heart tonight, may they die (the Germans, of course)." Reading these lines, written in the heat of the moment, and you realize just how complicated the path to reconciliation must have been after the war. The beginnings of European integration would have to wait until the anger, disgust, and violence had subsided.

One morning Sainto saw a young man lying on a straw mat in a makeshift shack. He must have been barely eighteen. Death was in his eyes. Petit Bob lifted his head, and the living ghost whispered, "It's all the same to me now. I can die in French arms, and I know my parents will recover my body." When the girls looked at each other, tears welled up in their eyes.

The road was interminable. The ambulances were directed toward Augsburg through fields of snow. The vehicles slid, skidded, crawled, to the great dismay of Petit Bob, who raged against them. She was tough, loyal, and stubborn, ready to give her all. When Sainto finally saw Augsburg, it was dark. But the commander of the place, a man named Ourens, who had been tipped off that they were coming, had pulled out all the culinary stops for them with the means at hand—a little corned beef, a few potatoes. But what was in the glasses was another matter. Miraculously, Ourens had found champagne—and cognac. Mouths warmed, cheeks rosy, the travelers went to bed with a small flame of joy.

The next day, in the dreariness of a winter that didn't seem to end, they went to a triage center. Sainto turned to Pagès: "You see? No doctor, no nurse. How can they do anything?"

"That's why we're here, Sainto. Let's get to it."

"Let's get to it."

And so, wearing their heavy US Army jackets, that's what they did. Their movements were clumsy, because of the cold and their thick sleeves, and yet precise. Dozens of Frenchmen were on hand to receive first aid. Infected wounds were cleaned, limbs were stitched and

Figure 6.1 Jeanine Robert, known to all as "Petit Bob," in an undated photograph, vivacious, with a wicked sense of humor. She partnered on the same ambulance with Simone Saint-Olive, "Sainto," who wrote in her journal, "I can only thank God for having put her in my path."

bandaged. Medicines were in short supply. Scalpels and needles were barely sterilized with burning alcohol. But the men didn't complain. They'd come back from hell, and the nurses could read the gratitude in their eyes. Tschupp filled in the forms that would enable the unfortunate men to be repatriated, but she knew their ordeal wasn't over yet. Most of them, when they arrived at the Gare du Nord with their haversacks and packs, would find nobody to welcome them. She'd seen many such young men in Paris wandering around, lost, shocked at the very sight of the street, all those buses, passersby, bakeries, crosswalks with their zebra patterns, three-wheeled carts. They saw life going on and they see that life went on, while they, carrying catastrophe inside them, destroyed from within, unable to tell their stories, were searching for their way home, where often no one was there anymore.

Pagès closed the eyes of a man wounded by a grenade.

Then they hit the road again, heading for Munich, and from there, they took the long drive back over the border to France to deliver some men whose condition was too fragile for the regular convoys. "We roll on, I give an injection to a man riding with us, I talk," Sainto noted. "Petit Bob drives very well. I can fill my syringes without any difficulty."

"You know what my most moving memory is?" Petit Bob said. "When we crossed the Rhine singing the Marseillaise. Silly, isn't it?"

Behind her, in the ambulance, a survivor was having an epileptic seizure. He could die. Petit Bob accelerated despite the slippery road. She wasn't afraid, this young woman who'd had to wait until she reached the age of majority to join the Red Cross. Her family had strictly forbidden her to do that, even though they were a patriotic family—the father and the grandfather had fought in World War I. But they must have felt she was too young.

Over the course of their missions and the miles that followed, the young women got to know each other. Even if the team in each vehicle was always the same, they got together with the other teams whenever they could, to chat, to forget for a moment the pain and suffering they encountered on a daily basis. All of them were young, under thirty, and all were driven by an impressive determination. They were not there by chance, but motivated by a desire to help, to participate, to "do their duty," as they modestly put it.

Jacqueline Heiniger, for example, took part in the Normandy campaign. After D-Day, she cared for wounded soldiers, evacuating some in conditions worthy of a novel. She came from a rural family in Lorraine. Her parents owned a cheese factory. From the age of sixteen, between four and five in the morning, she traveled the countryside, behind the wheel of a truck, to collect milk directly from the farms. When her work was done, she got on her bike and rode to the station to catch the train to Dijon, where she studied accounting at a business school. The war changed her life, but those circumstances helped bring out her altruistic and determined character.

Aline Tschupp, known simply by her surname, has a somewhat similar background. Coming from a modest family in Alsace, the youngest of five children, she developed a particular sensibility to the difference in treatment between girls and boys. On her own, she learned to swim at the municipal swimming pool and went cross-country skiing with friends, something unusual for a girl of her background. She learned English and took up photography as an apprentice to a professional. After training as a nurse, she became governess to the children of the Count and Countess de La Rochefoucauld, with whom she stayed until she joined the Red Cross at the end of the war. It was the Count who taught her to drive, a skill she was to put to good use on the roads of Eastern Europe.

I can't help but envy them, these young women who knew my aunt so well. They all rave about her when they talk about her, and I'm tempted to see in each of them a reflection of what Madeleine was. Their smiles, bright, frank, and luminous—their dedication, their energy. When you see them in the photos, you want to get to know them. They look good in their uniforms, and their spontaneous poses show their good nature.

At the start of the mission in Germany, the crews took turns evacuating the wounded they found on their route. They gave them first aid, and then covered mile after mile, day and night, to bring them back to France. Gradually, they moved deeper into Germany, pushing their search ever farther, following the progress of the Seventh American Army.

Farther and farther, until one day . . .

Chapter 7

HELL
(April 29, 1945)

What struck them was the silence. There was not a sound, not a bird singing, not an insect whirring, not a single human voice. Only the April wind and the tall grass seemed to be alive. American military trucks, stamped with the white star, waited. An American soldier, sitting on a crate in front of a courtyard, rifle on the ground, head down, cried. In front of him, a skeletal corpse with a shaved head was frozen in the posture in which death has seized him, one hand outstretched, the other resting on a stone.

The five ambulances of the Blue Squadron, led by Guillot, rolled slowly to a halt in front of the first barracks. Tschupp got out first, followed by Pagès, Sainto, Petit Bob, Reveron, Blaise, and Stiffler. A fine dust rose beneath their feet. They realized it was not dust, but human ashes.

Barracks lined up in tight rows at KL Dachau (Konzentrationslager Dachau), the longest-running and one of the largest of the thousands of prison camps and extermination centers set up during the twelve years of Nazi rule in Germany. It was initially a camp for political enemies of the Nazis, socialists, labor union leaders, communists, and others, including French opponents of the Vichy regime. Over time, it expanded to others whose existence contradicted the Nazis' vision of their Aryan utopia, including Roma people, Jehovah's Witnesses, gay men, and Jews, sent there mainly for forced labor, though many thousands were executed, or sent to extermination camps elsewhere, or simply died as a result of the

49

extreme brutality of the camp regime, where execution was the common punishment for almost any infraction.

What they saw was unimaginable to the young women of the Blue Squadron. At the far end of the camp from where they entered was the main building, some one hundred meters long, now housing the health services and administrative centers of the US Army, which had come from Munich, fifteen kilometers away, so close to the evil epicenter of Nazism.

The camp was huge. A few able-bodied prisoners had been evacuated before April 29, the date of the camp's liberation, but that was too late for some. Charles Delestraint, a lieutenant-general and a Resistance leader captured during the Occupation, was executed at Dachau by the SS at the beginning of April. "The most astonishing thing," Sainto recalled with great emotion, "is that the last convoys to arrive here left Compiègne, Lyon and Bordeaux in July and August 1944, by which time the D-Day landings had already taken place and Allied troops were advancing. The militia, the collaborators, the SS, the bastards did everything they could to speed up their operations. The last months of the war were the heaviest in terms of human losses."

A typhus epidemic, which still raged, had decimated the survivors. Sainto, without speaking, pointed to the barracks. The eleven young women headed for the dormitories. A terrible, haunting smell of death hung in the air. A mound of ashes and human remains formed a hill weighing several tons. It was the slag heap of death.

Within the camp grounds, a rail convoy of thirty-nine locked wagons from the Buchenwald camp had not been opened by the SS. Two thousand four hundred corpses were discovered inside them. The SS camp commandant was on the run.

There were around four thousand inmates. Typhus took a hundred of them every day. The squadron had to act fast. The girls made their way up the rows of beds, where skinny men with eyes that ate into their faces gazed at the visitors. Outside, through the window, they could see the last corpses, already sprinkled with lime. It was a terrible sight: torsos with ribs sticking out, mouths open in a last scream, eyes hollowed out and devoured by vermin, stomachs swollen, limbs green. The stench of burned flesh mingled with the smell of decay forced the rare American soldiers who passed by to hold handkerchiefs under their noses.

The girls, eyes reddened, jaws clenched, tended to the living. For the dead, they could do nothing, not even evacuate them. On the thin blankets in the dormitory, pinned papers showed the number, name, and country of each prisoner. The American authorities hesitated: what to do with all these men? There were thirty thousand of them when the GIs arrived, many of them with no family, sometimes no country, and more often than not, no home. General Patton proposed keeping them in camps, though simple humanity demanded that the barbed wire be taken away, and it was.

The nurses' gestures were precise, their movements as economical as possible. There was no question of wasting time or energy. Every minute counted. A man on a bench opened his eyes.

"Are you French?" he asked.

Sainto takes his hand. He was little more than a bundle of bones, and he was cold. "From Lyon."

The man struggled for breath.

"Will you say a Mass for me?"

"We'll get you out of here."

But even God wouldn't be able to do anything for this man. Besides, where was God in this place, where hundreds of priests had been murdered, more than eight hundred of them from Poland but many also from France. Their crimes? Resisting the Nazis or helping Jews. Among the survivors who witnessed the atrocities at Dachau was Mgr. Gabriel Piguet, the bishop of Clermont-Ferrand who hid Jewish children at a Catholic boarding school in Clermont-Ferrand and was arrested in 1944 for hiding a priest wanted by the Nazis. He is listed among the Righteous Gentiles at Yad Vashem, the Holocaust memorial in Jerusalem.

We had to keep going.

Outside, a scream. One of the Blue Squadron girls held her hands over her mouth. Later, Sainto would recount, "In the huge kennels, there are other corpses, those of the police dogs trained to catch runaways."

The girls pulled themselves together. They set about caring for the shivering patients. Fever reigned. For hours on end, they devoted themselves to the task, their souls dead and their hearts full of rage. Finally, as the afternoon wore on, an American doctor came to see them. His eyes were sky-blue, and he spoke with a Boston accent.

"How are you getting on?"

"Thank you, Major. We're short of medicine, especially morphine. Do you have anything to tide us over?"

"Not right now. In a few days, I think."

They left. Heiniger lit a cigarette. The horror seemed frozen on her face even though she was no stranger to horror. She'd seen some tough cases during the D- Day landings. Sainto turned to Major Bedell.

"How is this possible?"

"It's not."

"How do you get people to understand this, in Paris or Washington?"

"We made films and have taken photos. See that guy over there throwing up? That's the photographer. Everything will be transmitted and archived."

The Americans had indeed, done a great deal to ensure that the memory of what happened was not lost. In the archives, which can now be consulted easily thanks to the internet, we can see the films and photos that Bedell spoke of. All those who saw places like Dachau wanted to bear witness to them. Because the unimaginable, the absolute horror, must not be allowed to happen again. We must tell; we must show! Himmler inaugurated Dachau in 1933, explained the American officer to the dismayed young women. At first, there were only Soviets, homosexuals, and Roma people. Then, during the war, the numbers and origins of the prisoners grew. Three hundred thousand victims passed through the camp. When the SS learned that Allied troops were approaching, they went on a killing spree. For the Jews, the worst period was from June 1944 to April 29, 1945, when the camp was liberated by the US Army.

What the Americans discovered when they entered the camp was so shockingly unbearable that the soldiers immediately executed some of the camp guards belonging to the SS, shooting them on sight. No one could have stopped them. The Nazis mixed up everything—common law criminals, communists, politicians, homosexuals, Jews—in the hope that they would kill each other. This also encouraged snitching. There was a sorting out among inmates. The *kapos* would start fights, beating people with leather straps, murdering some of them. They would force inmates to kneel down and hold a bowl of soup on their outstretched arms. Whoever spilled a drop was immediately killed. Similar methods of finding a reason to kill were widespread throughout the camps. The Nazis' reasoning was racial, as well as economic. A working Jew brought in 1,620 marks a month. The calculation was simple: he cost the camp 180 marks a month and was rented out to Mercedes or Volkswagen or some other industrial company. The only problem was the corpses. There were too many. They couldn't burn them all or make big enough pits. Plus, the prisoners had to be kept under surveillance, with men and dogs.

The Blue Squadron girls turned pale as they heard more.

The dogs were there to tear apart people who were trying to get through the barbed wire. It is said that that's how Stalin's son Yakov, a prisoner in Sachsenhausen, died. When the Nazis proposed an exchange for Friederich Paulus, the German field marshal taken prisoner by the Russians when he surrendered at Stalingrad in 1942, Stalin refused. "You don't exchange a soldier for a marshal," he said. Yakov threw himself on the electric fence and was eaten by the dogs.

"What's that building over there at the end?"

"That's the SS infirmary."

"Can we use it?"

"I wouldn't recommend it. It was a torture center. Next door was a Nazi brothel."

All felt the same disgust.

The day ended with a sad tally: among the French, though relatively few in number, the dead were adding up fast. A priest, Abbé de La Martinière, vicar of Gien, stayed behind to help. A French Resistance fighter, Walter Bassan, had already left for Paris, along with a writer, Robert Antelme, in whose book, *L'Espèce Humaine, The Human Species*, he described human experience reduced to "naked life." Sainto noted in her diary, "Many of these pale-cheeked ghosts, these stunted old men of thirty, with limbs like weathervanes, are no more in spirit than stammering, broken children, who cry when spoken to, and whose souls are as fragile as their bodies. The crime against these souls is the Nazis' most inexpiable crime. But it's up to us to get these men, all these men, out of this hell immediately, and slowly, patiently, restore them to their dignity as free men."

The next day, the camp commandant, an American, carried out the decision he'd made the moment he entered this cursed place. He attended the arrival of a handful of residents of Munich, good Germans "who knew nothing, nothing about nothing." These people, bourgeois or aristocratic, fathers or veterans of the two wars, women or men, were forced to pick up shovels and bury the corpses.

In the early days, upon discovering the massacres committed in their name, some of these visitors committed suicide on their way home.

The girls of the Blue Squadron stood among the American soldiers who had come to watch the arrival of the Germans. It was like a guard of honor, only dishonorable. The GIs' faces were hard, and you could tell they want to wipe the place clean.

"I understood them," Sainto told me. "It's hard to renounce revenge."

There were two large women in the group who were furious at being rounded up for cleaning work. You could sense their conviction that they were in the right, that they were a superior breed.

When they reached the pile of corpses, they turned pale.

One of them fainted.

One of the soldiers there, hatred in his eyes, twisted his cap in his hands. He was clearly beside himself. Petit Bob looked at him and asked what was going on. The GI turned to her to say something, but he was at a loss for words. Petit Bob knows that just before the camp was liberated, the Nazis began evacuating prisoners to other concentration camps in endless, pointless death marches. When some prisoners found the strength to escape, the good villagers combed the woods and finished them off.

Different country, same camps. It was Majdanek in Poland that Madeleine, for her part, was to discover with horror.

Chapter 8

STILL HELL

(May 1945)

The distance between Munich and Warsaw is over a thousand kilometers. In the best-case scenario, the women of the Blue Squadron wouldn't reach their final destination before the end of July. While they waited, the team in Poland has to continue its work. Ducroquet and Madeleine headed east, toward the border between Poland and the USSR.

In the distance, Madeleine could see a tall chimney rising to the sky. The Majdanek camp. The official name was "Konzentrationslager Lublin," given the camp's proximity to the Polish city. It was immense, several hundred hectares. It was to this place, Madeleine knew, that the Jews of the Warsaw ghetto were deported, to be exterminated, methodically. Madeleine, in her effort to collect information, had learned that the prisoners were employed as slaves in a nearby factory, Steyr Daimler, and she remembered a trip she once made to Alsace in a truck built by Daimler. She shuddered. Ducroquet had been driving for hours, his face marked by fatigue. The one hundred and fifty kilometers separating Warsaw from Majdanek had been appalling. They had been followed by an all-terrain UAZ, the Soviet version of the American Jeep, for the entire route. Soviet army checks were frequent—and aggressive. It was as if the Russian soldiers lived in a state of permanent rage—or permanent hangover. The road, in very poor condition, put the ambulance's axles to a severe test. In the distance, slow-moving trains passed by, sometimes emitting a long wail. Passing through ransacked villages, Madeleine and

Ducroquet saw makeshift markets, where old women sold their last possessions—a few iron buttons, an ink pen cap, shell casings.

They passed the high walls of a monastery. Madeleine couldn't help but think of the women, or the men, who still lived there. She knows that in devastated Poland, nuns were no better off than other women. For Russian soldiers, there was no respect for religion, and even worse: nuns were traitors, since they believed in a God who served to oppress the people. Few Polish nuns were seen in the streets; they tried to protect themselves by making people forget their existence. But soon, Madeleine would have the opportunity to meet some of them. It was an episode she wouldn't say anything about for a long time.

For her part, Madeleine had put God aside, something that didn't start with the war. She remembered having a naïve faith during her childhood, a faith tinged with the bourgeois obligation to make her first communion. Later, when she arrived in Paris, she distanced herself from churches. Her medical studies opened her up to another world, turning her away from beliefs and toward a more scientific understanding of life. And then the war and the horrors she discovered implanted in her the question: "But how could God, if He existed, allow this to happen?" She could no longer believe.

As she entered Majdanek, Madeleine thought of Heinrich Himmler, on whose orders the camp had been created. Himmler, the Reichsführer-SS, the man who commanded both the SS and the Gestapo—the paramilitary organization that enforced the Nazi dictatorship and the Secret Police that collected information on "enemies of the Reich,"—had committed suicide a few weeks before. In Majdanek, five hundred thousand people had been incarcerated over the years of the Third Reich, a hundred and fifty thousand of whom died here. Madeleine got out, and Ducroquet opened the ambulance doors. The Soviets had cleaned the place out, and it seemed almost deserted. Only a few sick people and a few survivors were present, waiting for . . . what?

They were not waiting for anything, really. The war had robbed them of everything. Prisoners from the Baltic states had become stateless; the Jews, German political prisoners, undesirables, were all wanderers with no place to go. Ducroquet pointed to mass graves, recently covered over.

"The Jews were exterminated here, by the SS, in November 1943," he says. "All the internees from camps in the region were regrouped here, and . . ."

But he didn't finish the sentence, and Madeleine and Ducroquet went back to the object of the mission, which was to find French nationals. The towering chimney dominated everything. You could see it wherever you were. There was no escaping it. Soviet officers headed for Madeleine and Ducroquet.

"Let's get going," Ducroquet said watching them approach. "The administrative phase. We'll have some fun with these gentlemen. It's going to take a while, but I've brought a few packs of American cigarettes."

And it did last for a while, but finally the formalities were complete. As Madeleine entered the French barracks, a young man stepped forward. He was twenty years old when he'd been deported for acts of resistance in occupied France. He was first interned at Auschwitz, then at Majdanek. He was a member of the Sonderkommando, the work unit made up of prisoners who were forced to do the grim dirty work of the camps. For ten months, he stuffed corpses into the crematoriums. That evening, Ducroquet recorded in his notebook the account given by this witness: "I was in charge with another deportee and under the supervision of a German of putting the corpses into the crematorium. They were all brought to us, dead during the night or on leaving the gas chamber. As we picked them up one at a time and placed them on a small cart, it sometimes happened that a body was still stirring, or even that the pseudo-dead person was complaining. The German would then finish him off, usually with a blow from his club. But on certain days, this scene was repeated several times. The gas chamber hadn't worked properly, or too many convicts had been introduced at once, and the concentration of gas wasn't lethal for all of them. We would then see whole series of unfortunates who had simply fainted, or even were still conscious, looking at us without speaking, others moaning, rambling or, worse still, realizing what was happening and begging us. Sometimes the German would knock them out, but when there were too many, he'd get angry and order us to stuff them into the oven as they were. If we hesitated, the blows of the club came down on us, along with the threat of being buried ourselves."

Madeleine and Ducroquet were stunned, both by what he said and by his detachment. "Intelligent boy, lively, helpful, not without distinction, very resourceful, daring, remained young and cheerful," Ducroquet wrote. At the bottom of the report, he added: "I've forgotten his name. I never knew his address. He was a Parisian." Madeleine understood as she continued to talk with him that he was in a secondary state. He was emotionless, shielded by a totally inexpressible pain. He has survived by shutting himself off so as not to feel anything. The writer Robert Antelme, deported to Dachau for acts of resistance, put it this way: "From the very first days, it seemed impossible to bridge the distance we discovered between the language we had and the experience that, for the most part, we were enduring in our bodies."

All the unfortunate Parisian can do was describe. He had forbidden himself to feel. It was a psychic death.

Having been liberated from the Nazis, he waited to go home—to Paris's Left Bank. Meanwhile, the young man drove a black Mercedes-Benz 170, whose Nazi pennant had been replaced by a small French embassy flag. The car belonged to the French embassy, and the young man was the embassy's chauffeur.

The few French people left behind at Majdanek were identified, cared for, and, once they were well enough, repatriated to France.

Madeleine was sent to Majdanek to report on camp operations. It wasn't the only time she'd received such an order from General Catroux in Moscow. Finding the telegrams in the archives of the Ministry of Foreign Affairs, I couldn't help thinking that sending a woman doctor was perhaps also a way of having a more discreet observer than a man would have been. In the collective imagination, a woman was there to heal, not to spy.

Despite the horror she felt, Madeleine set out to understand the inner workings of the camp. But she must also bear witness, learn everything she can, and what she learned was the bureaucratic functioning of the vast machinery of extermination, which followed a chilling set of procedures. Before the deaths described by the young Parisian, the deportees were stripped of their clothes. They had to undress in stages in different rooms. There was the men's suit room, the underwear room, the shoe room. "The most searingly moving," wrote Ducroquet "was that of children's shoes, where thousands of small sizes—shoes,

sandals, slippers—waited to be repaired by inmates before being sent
to the Œuvre de secours d'hiver, the Winter Relief Work [in German,
the Winterhilfswerk, the Nazi charity that distributed goods stolen from
Jews and other camp inmates to ordinary Germans]. Next is their hair,
which was made into felt. Then their teeth, if they're gold. This stage
normally comes after death, but the dentist sometimes prefers to pull the
teeth of the living . . . Finally, it's death and the crematorium."

When I was twenty, I took a trip to Poland with three other
students. Our journey took us through Krakow and across the river
to Auschwitz. I was petrified to discover the concentration camp. I'd
imagined a few barracks, like in Alain Resnais's film *Nuit et Brouillard,
Night and Fog*, which I'd seen at a screening at the high school film club.
But this was something else, this city of death, this universe organized in
a methodical, implacable way, to exterminate the individual. That day,
I touched Nazi barbarism with my fingertips. These are impressions and
feelings I'll never forget.

Madeleine stayed several days in Majdanek. Perhaps there were
French people in other nearby camps? It was necessary to scour the
territory. And quickly. Orders from Moscow were now very hostile. Catroux met Andrey Vychinski, Soviet foreign minister and a
close, many would say servile, advisor to Stalin, in an effort to secure
Russian cooperation, or at least acquiescence in the repatriation effort.
Vychinsky, Catroux recalled, was the chief prosecutor at the famous
Moscow show trials in the late 1930s, when he had many of his fellow
communists, now designated as traitors by Stalin, executed. You can't
expect anything from a man like that, but you have to try. Catroux
tried but achieved nothing. The Lublin Committee, set up by Moscow
as an alternative to the government in exile in London, gave way to the
Provisional Government of National Unity, the next step in the Soviet
effort to outmaneuver the non-communist London group and hand
power in Poland to its pro-Moscow puppets.

Meanwhile, at the Allied summit in Yalta in February, Roosevelt
and Churchill agreed to Stalin's demand that Poland's borders be shifted
westward, to the gain of the victorious Soviet Union and the loss of
defeated Germany. The country's former easternmost territory would go
to the Soviet Union, and all the former German territory in the west, up
to the Oder-Neisse line, would belong to the new Poland. The move,

Roosevelt told Congress when, exhausted, haggard, and pale, he got home from Yalta, was "to help create a strong independent, and prosperous nation . . . with a government ultimately to be selected by the Polish people themselves." In fact, what history has shown is that both Roosevelt and Churchill felt they had no choice but to yield to Stalin on the Polish question. "To put it more brutally," Arthur Bliss Lane, the American ambassador to Poland, later wrote, Yalta "was a capitulation on the part of the United States and Great Britain," one that essentially gave to Stalin what he'd gained when he and Hitler had divided Poland between the two of them in 1939—and then gave up when Hitler attacked in 1941 and Stalin was desperate for Western aid. Later also, as Bliss Lane reports, the president of the Polish-American Congress wrote that Roosevelt was "outwitted, outmaneuvered, and outfoxed by Stalin." In short, while few in the West realized this at the time, the Iron Curtain was falling across Europe, starting at the new Oder-Neisse line.

And yet, on May 8, all over Europe, there was an explosion of joy.

The Germans surrendered; the war was over, well over. In Paris, the jubilation was total, the streets overrun by delirious crowds. American soldiers were covered in flowers and kissed by adoring girls; windows were open; French flags were flying in the wind; people were dancing, singing, crying, hugging, kissing, talking, drinking. So much fear, so much suffering; so many nights, so many deaths, and now it was all coming to an end. . . . These simple words—the war is over—were enough to light up the world. In London, Helsinki, Athens, Tunis and Stockholm, life tasted better. In Moscow, vodka flowed freely; the "Little Father of the People," Uncle Joe Stalin, was celebrated by millions of subjects. Five years of the worst darkness of the human soul had come to an end.

Chapter 9

DYING FOR DANZIG

(May 25–June 2, 1945)

A few weeks after her arrival in Warsaw, Madeleine stopped taking notes in her diaries. There was no more time for that. She nonetheless wrote some reports ordered by the office of General de Gaulle, by the Ministry of Foreign Affairs, and by Ambassador Garreau directly—no doubt because it was hard for him to move about the country himself, given his role as French representative. It would have been an indiscretion to do that, and anyway, for a diplomat to travel required special authorization—in contrast to the Red Cross, which was generally able to move about the country.

Politically, the situation was murky. The government-in-exile in London was trying to get itself recognized by the Western powers, while the newly formed Provisional Government of the Republic of Poland, made up largely of members of the former Lublin Committee, was gaining ground. France officially favored the creation of a Poland that would be a buffer between a permanently weakened Germany and the Soviet Union, which was becoming more worrisome by the day, and like the United States and Britain, had recognized the Provisional Government, which was supposed to be only temporarily in power, pending national elections. But this was a fiction only partially disguising the Soviet moves to ruthlessly suppress whatever remained of a non-communist resistance. Already, the Russians had liquidated the Polish Army of the Interior, the Home Army, which had led the wartime resistance against the Germans. Twenty of its leaders were shot to death or hung, and fifty thousand were arrested. The Soviet Union was slowly, brutally, consolidating its power over Poland.

Under the circumstances, it was necessary for Madeleine to work nonstop, while it was still possible. Finding the French citizens lost in the turbulence depended on word of mouth, on information coming from the migrations of people always in flux. She had to go places, to see what was happening in recently liberated cities and towns, to take the pulse, to keep looking, to keep looking.

And so, in May 1945, when the head of the Polish Red Cross, Ludvig Christians, suggested that Madeleine accompany him on a trip to Danzig, she readily accepted. A former German territory, given to Poland in the Treaty of Versailles so it would have access to the sea, Danzig had been liberated—or "taken," as Madeleine put it in her reports—rather late by the Russians, in the middle of March. The Red Cross itself was in total chaos. Its president, General Stanislaw Szeptycki, who was the hero of the 1920 battle of Warsaw against the new Russian Bolshevik regime, had resigned, and every day the experienced members of the association were being replaced by communists who knew nothing of the terrain. The Russian ambassador in Warsaw, Viktor Lebedev, actively supported this takeover. The worried Catholic hierarchy was pleading with the ambassador of the United States, Arthur Bliss Lane: "Don't let the Polish people be crucified."

But Bliss Lane had never confronted such a situation: a battered and devastated country emerging from a barbaric wartime domination only to be threatened by another nominally peaceful nation that was threatening an equally ruthless domination. He had been the second secretary in the US Embassy in Warsaw in 1919–1920 and knew the country well. Before going to Poland, he'd had a long diplomatic career, posted, among other places, to Nicaragua, Lithuania, and Yugoslavia, a consummate diplomatic professional who, in 1947, resigned his post in protest to what he saw as American passivity in the face of Soviet atrocities. During his time in Poland, starting in 1945, he lived in what remained of Warsaw's Polonia Hotel, a grand six-story structure that vaguely resembled the Lutetia in Paris. Polonia was the only building still standing in the ruined field that had once been the vital center of Warsaw, though it was studded with shards. There was a good reason the building had survived: until the last minute, the Polonia had been the headquarters of the Wehrmacht and the SS in Warsaw, just as the Lutetia had been in Paris.

Looking out the window of his bedroom, Bliss Lane saw a desert, "a study in despair . . . mute testimony to the barbarity of Nazi policy, unjustified by any military or strategic reason." Inside the Polonia, one of the few buildings that had electricity, it was relatively warm and comfortable. "Outside were ragged men and women and children—hunger, illness and cold. . . . But the most terrible sight of all was that of the children amputees. They were those whose legs or arms were carried away by bombs, or whose gangrene-affected limbs had been amputated to save their lives. It was heart-breaking to observe how the war had left these frail victims everywhere in Europe. In Warsaw we counted them in sickening numbers. . . . They hobbled, on crutches made of such sticks as they could find, to open the doors of the few automobiles, and silently held out their hands" (Bliss Lane, *I Saw Poland Betrayed*, 21–22).

In the city itself, all that remained of the former central railway station was two columns emerging from the burned earth. The streets no longer conformed to the map. "It is probably the only town in Europe, perhaps even in the world, of more than a million inhabitants whose population dwindled at a certain point in history down to nought—well, perhaps to 150, fugitives hiding in the cellars and ruins on the left bank of the river." Or so wrote Olgierd Budrewicz, the Polish writer and journalist. Nineteen forty-five was Warsaw year zero.

But Bliss Lane could also see Warsaw starting to rise from the ashes. The populace's desire to live was strong. When he walked in the old historic heart of the city (his car, which had been requisitioned by the Nazis during his wartime absence, couldn't be driven on what was a pile of jagged stones), he talked to people. He wanted to help the children. But what to do when you're constantly under the eyes of the men in leather jackets? Bliss Lane was under constant surveillance by the Russians themselves or their Polish collaborators, who were aiding the communists in tightening their grip. The few Westerners in the city all knew each other, and the ambassador was well aware of Pauliac's efforts to help these unfortunate children. Maybe one day, there would be an occasion for him to do something for her, with her.

Madeleine described her Danzig expedition in her report to de Gaulle. They went in two trucks, Pauliac together with Christians of the Polish Red Cross and Captain Birckel, her Polish translator. They left at 8 a.m., and almost immediately, they were in the Polish dystopia. "The road was in a poor state, all the bridges on the Vistula had been destroyed," Pauliac wrote. "We drove through Grudziadz, which was partially damaged, and everywhere we started to see burned tanks, destroyed automobiles, abandoned pontoon boats and felled trees"—no doubt for firewood during the freezing winter just past.

"We soon encountered two strange caravans," Pauliac continued, "each made of about a hundred Polish farming carts, equipped with tarpaulins meant to protect their occupants at night and filled with an incongruous sort of bric-a-brac—huge mirrors, gold-fringed curtains, horn loudspeakers, furniture. . . . The carts, all led by Russian women who'd been liberated from the German camps, each had a dozen horses attached to them, not including the many foals roaming freely around them. They were all headed south, in complete chaos, without having a precise notion of left or right, creating huge clouds of dust and blocking the roads, causing a stir and utter discontent."

On the road, the small Red Cross convoy passed Russian soldiers taking away entire herds of cattle. The Russians drove the animals everywhere, trampling fields just pushing up with new wheat, which horrified the passengers in the two trucks. Polish agriculture was on the verge of recovering when the Soviets imposed a supposed agrarian reform that the propaganda said would bring new bounty to the near-starving country, but in fact, it was akin to the disastrous collectivization of agriculture that it had carried out in the 1930s in the Soviet Union itself, and it threatened to ruin Polish farming completely. The spring planting had been done, but, as a Foreign Ministry report put it, nobody knew how the harvest would be accomplished, because horses, bulls, and cows had been "requisitioned" by the Russians.

Madeleine's trip to Danzig had an official purpose, to search for furniture and medical supplies for the hospital in Warsaw. She had been informed that some of both could be found in a hospital on the German submarine base in Danzig, seized by the Russians two months earlier. But that was a cover for the unofficial purpose of the trip, which was the usual one of collecting information on French citizens trapped in northern Poland and finding ways of getting them home.

The village of Toruń, situated halfway between Warsaw and Danzig, was intact. Arriving at the Red Cross office there, Pauliac and Captain Birckel learned there was a camp about ten kilometers away that had been evacuated just the night before in the direction of Stettin. Birckel went to the camp to check if anyone was left and found five hundred French still there. At the time, the Soviets had allowed thousands of French citizens to be repatriated from Odessa on the Black Sea coast, where ships took them back to France, though first they had to spend time in a Russian transit camp. But rumors were rife that the Odessa passage was unsafe, with some of the ships sinking, and the five hundred men discovered by Birckel, apparently believing the rumors, had refused to go to the Russian camp, preferring to wait for the route through Berlin to open up, which, in turn, depended on the war finally ending.

Meanwhile, at Red Cross headquarters, Madeleine came across twenty-two Frenchmen who were staying there. These men had taken on new lives for themselves, finding work—one, for example, was a barber, another a baker. Most of them had been rounded up in the *Service du Travail Obligtoire*, the Compulsory Labor Service, the Germans ordering them onto farms in Pomerania in order to work in the fields (freeing up Germans to go into the front). Many of them were taken back to France, but some of them had married Polish women, and the new Lublin authorities refused to allow the Polish wives of these Frenchmen to follow their husbands to France, so some of the Frenchmen had opted to stay with their wives. It was a difficult decision, but there was no other option for these couples.

Toruń itself hadn't been damaged. Its façades, typical of Hanseatic cities, were beautiful, with their rows of stepped roofs. After so much ruin, it was good to see a town still standing. In the center was a monument to the Poles sacrificed in the World War I battles that had taken place on the French front—the Chemin des Dames, the Marne, Bar le Duc, the Somme, Verdun.

A ceremony was held in the town hall, where Red Cross officials presented the Poles with several crates of medicine. Toasts were exchanged, and glasses were raised. Then, as the mayor congratulated the visitors, all eyes turned toward the entry, where some nuns led a group of young girls—orphans, according to Birckel—who offered flowers to Madeleine, and then, to the strains of *la Marseillaise*, sung by both the Poles and the French, she continued on her mission.

La Marseillaise—it had always had an emotional impact on Madeleine. She was a member of the French generation growing up during a time of a highly developed, post–Great War cult of patriotism, one centered on an almost-religious love of the Republic. Her father, after all, had given his life for France, and her family revered his memory. Like her sister, Anne-Marie, Madeleine still remembered how the *Marseillaise* was sung every day in the school courtyard.

The rest of the trip wasn't so folkloric. The Vistula bridges had been destroyed, and the roads were congested with refugees—women, men, and children perched on carts, traveling in a state of complete anarchy, indifferent to the rules of the road, moving with the wind, it seemed, some of them escaping from the east as it fell under the Soviet yoke, others coming from the west, trying to recover their land. These poor wretches crisscrossed each other, exhausted and without any means to feed themselves, haggard men and women in an end-of-the-world landscape. Near Danzig, convoys of German prisoners crossed the convoy's path. They were ragged, a lot of them barefoot, resigned, worn out, guarded by a small number of Russian soldiers. Pauliac almost felt pity for them, except that the memory of the Majdanek concentration camp was still fresh in her mind.

The closer the truck got to Danzig, the more checkpoints there were, the Russians inspecting the load each time, looking for alcohol. "We were stopped at four Russian checkpoints," Madeleine later wrote. "It was pointless to try to explain at checkpoints two, three, and four that checkpoint one had already opened a suitcase, trampled a bag, and completely disorganized our studiously arranged luggage. We had to go through the same ordeal each time, and the fact that we were French citizens or Red Cross workers made no difference." When the first truck finally arrived in Danzig, the second truck was nowhere in sight. Later it turned out that the Russians had stopped it and kept it from going on all night, its passengers spending the hours curled up on their seats, hoping that their misadventure would come to an end with the dawn.

Danzig, a major port on the Baltic Sea, was another of Poland's cities ruined during the war; it was also a symbol of Poland's turbulent and tragic history. It was Polish in the Middle Ages, known as Gdansk, but it was annexed by Prussia after the eighteenth-century partition of Poland and was part of newly unified Germany until Germany's defeat in World War I. When Poland regained its independence after the war, Danzig became a free city, a sort of semi-state. It was the first territory attacked by the Nazis when they invaded Poland (in agreement with the Soviet Union) in 1939. During the war, it was bombarded, first by the Germans, then by the Russians. Half of the city's Jewish population escaped before 1939, but the half that didn't was rounded up and massacred by the Nazis. In 1944 and 1945, as the Russians advanced, thousands of Germans, now refugees, descended on the port city, trying to board ships to escape to the West. Many of these refugees were killed in the attempt; many remained behind as refugees when the Russians took over.

When Madeleine arrived in May, the city, now once again given its Polish name, Gdansk, had been returned to Polish control, but the communists, supported by the Russians, were in charge. Like Warsaw, it was a ruin. When the Germans retreated from the city, they let it be known that if they couldn't keep it, nobody could, and they destroyed everything, as they had in Warsaw, house by house, including the magnificent Saint Elisabeth Cathedral. After that, as Madeleine's colleague on the Polish Red Cross, Ludwig Christians, observed bitterly, "The Russians, when they arrived, finished the job."

The spectacle was Dantesque. Nothing still stood in this martyr of a city. "It's only piles of ruins and carcasses of houses," Madeleine noted. "Only a few streets are passable." They saw cadavers in the canals, and many more were still buried under the rubble of collapsed houses, such that "the smell in some streets is unbearable," Madeleine wrote. "All that is left are the remains of the city gates of the Rathaus [the city hall]. Some streetcars have been knocked over or burned. They still bear the German inscription, 'Ohne Kampf kein Sieg' [No struggle no victory] in big letters." And the traces of that struggle were everywhere: trenches, anti-tank hedgehogs, barricades constructed out of trees. A recently liberated Frenchman explained to Pauliac that everything had been done by French prisoners during bombing raids, under the threat of guns, practically without food. A lot of men had died constructing these flimsy defenses against Russian tanks.

Madeleine's delegation found accommodations a few miles from the town, in a branch office of the Red Cross, where between sixty and a hundred twenty refugees were lodged and fed each day—a remarkable achievement given the meager resources available. The day after her arrival, word having gotten around that she was there, Madeleine received a visit from some nuns from a nearby convent. They had come despite the great danger; Russian soldiers targeted women, pillaging, raping, and killing with sickening regularity. Madeleine closeted herself with the nuns to hear their story. Others came to see her, with similar tales. "The surgeon at the hospital in Gydnia told me that he repaired the perineums of young rape victims every day," Madeleine wrote in her report to Garreau. "A Frenchman at the Chichau camp, working in a Polish maternity ward, told me how the Russians came every day and raped women who'd just given birth or who were about to give birth. Every night, the Russians came back and there were fights over possession of the women with wounded and dead." The Russians were animals, and there wasn't a virgin left within a circle of a hundred kilometers—he told Madeleine. And when they finished raping, the Russians pillaged and destroyed everything. They were on conquered territory, and they believed it all belonged to them. There were the spoils of war taken from the Germans, of course, but Polish goods were also fair game, too, in their eyes.

Every day, Madeleine found small French groups wandering in the vicinity. Thirteen came from a camp at Chichau and were under the orders of a sublieutenant named Bellangu, and a non-commissioned officer, Dupont. After the Germans left, these two had stayed in the camp to take care of the others. For ten days, there was nonstop bombing. Though not doctors, they took care of as many of the men as they could, night and day. When the bombing stopped, they got help from an Italian doctor to set up a sort of dispensary, where they treated everybody who needed it. They, too, had their complaints about the Russians. Not only did they rape and steal, but they did so even after they'd been cared for medically. Bellangu had to retrieve his jacket when the man whose wounds he'd sewed up tried to take it away.

"The day after my arrival," Madeleine wrote in her report, "a delegation of five German Catholic nuns working for the Red Cross came to see me. There had been twenty-five originally; fifteen were dead—raped and killed by the Russians. Five of the ten remaining were pregnant."

In a dystopic universe where all the normal moral signposts had been destroyed, Madeleine was, nonetheless, not the only person who retained a sense of humanity. She met another Frenchman, Henri Boyer, a former medical student who in his third year had been impressed into the STO, the Obligatory Labor Service. After working in a bakery in Germany, he was sent to a hospital in Langfuhr, a suburb of Danzig. There, he became a surgeon, and he stayed after the war ended, aware of his usefulness. Happy to come across a compatriot, he told Madeleine what it had been like.

After the Russians took the city, they brought in their wounded. An officer was always present when they were being treated, his revolver in his hand, threatening to kill everybody if one of the wounded men died. One day, when Boyer and a German nun, a nurse, were treating a patient, a Russian officer arrived, ordered Boyer to leave at gunpoint, whereupon he raped the nun.

Boyer had seen too much. He wanted the atrocities to be known, not to remain in the shadows, and he wanted Pauliac as a witness. He led her out onto the former Adolph-Hitler-Strasse, walking carefully because the Germans had mined the roads when they retreated, as evidenced by the burned-out tanks they saw. Madeleine followed the young man into an old warehouse, not asking any questions, but hesitating when she understood what he wanted to show her.

"There were great barrels with about a hundred human bodies in them, decapitated—the heads were in other barrels," she wrote later. "One of the bodies bore the tattoos of a Polish sailor, another had 'class of 1912' tattooed on his arm."

This lugubrious scene (also witnessed and described by Petit Bob when she was in Gdansk some time later) was a soap factory, the soap made from human bodies and then used in the operating rooms.

Despite these horrors, Pauliac had to keep her mind on the practical purpose of the trip to Danzig, which was to search for furniture, linens, and dishes to bring to the French Hospital in Warsaw. Roger Garreau had given her a letter of introduction to the *voivode*, or district chief, of Danzig-Gdansk, who gave her a cordial reception on May 30. Not far away, in Gdynia, where there was a hospital, Pauliac had discovered some Frenchmen, some of them wounded in bombings, others simply waiting for somebody to come and find them. After she'd collected their identities, they wanted to know the following:

"Is it true that America has declared war on Russia?"
"And what about the Odessa transports? Have they really sunk?"
"It seems that there have been fifteen thousand dead."

Madeleine assured them that none of this was true. She continued to encounter others who'd heard the same rumors and asked the same questions.

Pauliac left Gdansk under perilous, yet ultimately fortuitous circumstances. The trucks were out of gas, and Pauliac had found no way to get any, despite numerous efforts. The *voivode* recommended that she see the Russian commander and ask him for gas. The general received her. "The gas is in Baku," he explained, referring to the capital of Azerbaijan. "And as far as I'm concerned," he added, "I'm just a guest in this country, the same as you. We are both on Polish territory."

Pauliac managed to keep her composure.

"I came to make a courtesy call on you," she said, "but coming into the city I was made to get out of my truck four times and my bags were searched each time. The soldiers who did that were Russians, and they didn't give the impression that they thought of themselves as guests here."

This exchange apparently caused some annoyance in the Russian hierarchy. Returning to her quarters, Madeleine found an orderly waiting for her. Michal Rola-Zymierski, a former Polish agent in the NKVD who had just been named marshal of Poland by Stalin, making him the most exalted person in the country, wanted to see her. She followed the orderly to the garden of Zymierski's residence together with his chief of staff—a Russian who spoke no foreign languages—and a female lieutenant from the propaganda department, and waited.

As she did so, Madeleine remembered what the marshal had declared the night before: in a statement to the press, Rola-Zymierski had complained that France wasn't behaving very well toward the Poles who had been liberated by the American army. This was a reference to the agreement signed in December 1944 requiring each country to allow foreigners to return to their original homes, and according to Rola-Zymierski, Poles who were in the territories controlled by the French were not being repatriated. What Rola-Zymierski didn't say was that at least some of these Polish citizens were hesitant to go back to their Soviet-controlled country, fearing they would be deported farther to the east. Had Rola-Zymierski wanted to see Madeleine in order to raise this issue with her? She didn't know, but anticipating that the meeting risked being disagreeable, and tired of waiting, she finally walked out, returning to her quarters so as to go back to Warsaw.

She recounted all this in casual fashion in her report, as an aside, but it was no ordinary event. Summoned essentially by a figure anointed by Stalin himself, she nonetheless left without waiting for him to appear. It was a risky move, but Madeleine was a strong woman, and she believed you had to be bold.

In the end, it was thanks to Hewlett Johnson, the dean of Canterbury, that Madeleine was able to safely return to her base in Warsaw. The prelate, who was in Gdansk at that time, offered to take her back to Warsaw in his own plane, and Pauliac accepted with gratitude, even though she found the prelate too indulgent in his attitude toward the recently formed Polish communist government in Lublin. Indeed, Hewlett Johnson, known as the "red dean," was a strong supporter of Stalin. Only Madeleine returned by plane with him. The rest of the team, including Birckel, remained, and brought the trucks and equipment back to Warsaw.

But politics has its reasons, and in that early June, France didn't yet know which government to recognize. The June 29 agreement for the repatriation of prisoners of war and deportees had been signed, which ought to have made Madeleine's task much easier. But during this time, the Russians continued to advance their pawns on the Polish chessboard, which they knew they could do without decisive opposition from the Allies. Since the conference at Yalta in February 1945, it was clear that Roosevelt and Churchill didn't want to go to war over Poland. Poland's fate was sealed, and the obstacles faced both by Madeleine and the Blue Squadron, which was approaching the Polish border, were becoming harder and harder to surmount.

Chapter 10

WHEELS TURNING
BEFORE POLAND

(June–July 1945)

The Blue Squadron was forging its legend. The young women were on the road night and day, covering the miles to bring the wounded to safety and organize their repatriation. From Munich, near where the Dachau camp was located, they made nonstop round trips to bring freed prisoners back to France, almost four hundred kilometers each way, on poorly maintained roads. "The most afflicted of the deportees are in an indescribable state," Sainto noted. "They want to die in France." And this pushed the squadron to ignore their fatigue, to forget everything except to give one last measure of comfort to these men and women who had lived through the unspeakable. That was all they could do, and they did it with all their soul, all their courage. It was so intense that Sainto didn't have time to write in the ambulance logbook.

But every page would look the same.

Once Dachau was emptied, they moved a little farther east to look after the Czechs who had been locked up in Buchenwald, the prison camp near Weimar created in 1937. The Blue Squadron had received direct orders to divert from their main repatriation mission to treat Czech prisoners and help them get back to their country. After the German surrender, there was close cooperation between France and Czechoslovakia, whose western territory, the Sudetenland, was given, in history's most notorious example of appeasement, to Hitler in accordance with the Munich Agreement of 1938, signed by the prime ministers of Britain and France. Hitler then occupied the rest of Czechoslovkia in 1939, making a travesty of the deal ironed out at

73

Figure 10.1   The Blue Squadron resting beside their ambulances somewhere on the road. Despite the hardships they faced, these young women tried to keep up their spirits. It was the powerful bonds that sprang up between them that enabled them to keep going.

Munich. After the German defeat, the newly established French government under de Gaulle reestablished the country's traditionally large diplomatic establishment in Prague and resumed its active cooperation with the Czechs.

The Blue Squadron transported liberated Czech prisoners from near Weimar across to the border to Pilsen, where they were able to get medical treatment, and with that mission accomplished, the wheels of the five ambulances rolled on, returning to Germany and the search for French citizens still there. The eleven young women had been working together for two months now. Of course, the bonds between the members of each team in each ambulance were the strongest, but each return to base camp was an opportunity for them to talk and share their experiences. Despite the "hatred in their hearts" that Sainto says they felt when facing the horrors they discovered, they carried on. They knew what they had to do—rescue, heal, give comfort to anyone who needed it. At one point on the road, they came across a badly damaged American truck, with wounded soldiers inside. They stopped immediately and did what they could, bandaging and treating. Blaise's ambulance had to

Figure 10.2 Some of the Blue Squadron members posing in front of an ambulance with American soldiers in Germany in June 1945. The Blue Squadron members are, from left to right: Charlotte Pagès, Jeanine Robert (Petit Bob), Micheline Reveron, Jacqueline Heiniger, Aline Tschupp, Élizabeth Blaise, and Cécile Stiffler.

be emptied of its lighter casualties to load the more seriously wounded American soldiers. Pagès stayed with those left behind on the side of the road, waiting for the next rotation.

Starting at the end of June, the Squadron was based in Weimar, where it was hosted by the American army. One evening, an American major invited them to a party, where Sainto was approached by a man. She didn't know him, she thought.

"But, Simone, what are you doing here?"

She was taken aback. Who was this slender young man calling out to her, in French no less? The man insisted.

"It's me! It's me! Don't you recognize me?"

The voice! Of course, it was Claude! A friend from Lyon, as if from another life. Sainto was stunned. They'd taken classes together, but now he was unrecognizable. And, the American major who freed him from Buchenwald told her, he'd already gained back several kilos.

"I found him gaunt, starving, standing only by strength of nerve and will," the American said.

After her return to France, Sainto would note, "The whole period of liberation from the camps was a time when misery appeared to Petit Bob and me as unbearable. Will we be scarred for life? . . . It's possible. Those smoking ovens, that pestilential smell, and, above all, those men, all the same, impossible to recognize, even a friend."

Cécile Stiffler, another of the "Bleues," was in the same state of moral shock. Later, many years after the end of the war, those close to her would recount how much she had changed during those trying months of their mission. She was always cheerful and smiling in her life before, but she came back sad and reserved. She said little. Only snatches sometimes escaped her. She felt the same inability to tell her story, something many deportees would experience.

The silence of witnesses grips tightly. It's the silence that Dr. Liber's son told me about, the silence that my own mother kept for so many years, before she began, in bits and pieces, to tell what Madeleine had told her, and only her. Words reactivate suffering. What kept the group together, what bound them, was the friendship forged by a shared experience that nobody who wasn't there can quite understand. Nothing can weaken the strength of that bond, until the day they die. They understand each other with a gesture, a look. There's no need for explanations. The harshness of the time they lived reinforces their need for solidarity and fraternity. Some have faith, some don't, but they all know why they're here. It's humanity's last refuge.

Even in the midst of turmoil, it was a small world. Micheline Reveron, known as "Miche," has a discussion with Claude, the young man Sainto met from Lyon, and she realized that her fiancé, killed at the start of the Alsace campaign, was from the same class at Saint-Cyr, the French military academy. Emotion gripped them both. Coincidences are always signs of destiny, when you're so far from home.

Why and how did these young women commit themselves to their grim, often-heartrending task? Sainto carried with her the ideals of scouting, the will to serve, the spirit of mutual aid. For Petit Bob, it seemed to be a visceral attachment to the country, the country her father defended before her. She took the place of the patriotic son her father never had. Jacqueline Heiniger, "Heini," had the same energy and independence. She didn't wait for her parents' approval, either. Even before Germany and the Blue Squadron, she signed up as a driver for the Red Cross. Her motto: *Act!* Miche, on the other hand, had a very independent character and had always felt the need to "be useful." She therefore chose to study nursing, standing up to her parents. According to Petit Bob, Élisabeth Blaise was also a prodigy of dedication.

Their dedication was essential, especially given that everything they needed for their mission was in short supply, especially given the appalling state of health of the men they found. Their only hope was to get them to a hospital as quickly as possible. The roads were bad, the ambulances broke down, but there was no stopping them. The "Bleues" got their hands dirty, made the necessary repairs, and got back on the road.

On July 2, they made a hasty departure from Weimar. The Red Army had arrived ahead of schedule, and in accordance with the agreements made with the Soviets, the Allies made way for them. The Germans also hit the road, in a panic of uncertainty about how things were going to be with the Russians, who had a fearsome reputation. The scenes of exodus from the territories about to be occupied by the Russians were like the scenes the young women saw in France in 1940 as the Germans rolled in. The ambulance drivers loaded up a few distraught stragglers, but travel became more difficult than ever. On some roads, Russians in horse-drawn *troikas* prohibited passage. The autobahn was only accessible from the American zone, that is, Nuremberg.

Still, the kilometers rolled by; the Blue Squadron advanced. The road maps were not very accurate: one evening, as night fell, they ended up in a wasteland. They turned around. Where were they? Sainto, exhausted, lay down in the back of her vehicle while Petit Bob drove. As the ambulance ground ahead, she saw a sign through the trees: "Autobahn 250 meters." She pointed this out to Petit Bob, who nodded and replied, "You see, we're working on it, and you're sleeping!"

"But, no! We had to turn right."

"Shut up and go to sleep!"

They started again, but they really were lost. They retraced their route; then, when they managed to get onto the autoroute, they stopped in a garage. It was the middle of nowhere, but they decided to remain there for some rest. Guillot, the group leader, ordered that they leave at 6 a.m. The area was not very safe. But sleep was stronger than prudence. At 8 a.m. Blaise woke up, startled.

"Wake up, girls!"

They drove toward Laningen, a small village where three Frenchmen had been reported to be staying. While Tschupp collected the sick men, Stiffler, a cigarette in her mouth, cleaned her uniform. But the fabric was impregnated with petrol, and suddenly she was engulfed in flames. Her hair burned. Everyone rushed in. More fright than harm. Tschupp's eyebrows were singed, holes are burned in her "canadienne," her fur-lined jacket. But she was alright.

The team split up: Tschupp and Stiffler brought some wounded men across the border to Strasbourg, while Guillot, Miche, and Petit Bob headed to Salzburg, Austria. Their mission: to find valves for the ambulance motors. There were almost-otherworldly moments. On the road to Salzburg, some Americans offered the French girls a place to stay, and the "place" turned out to be an exquisite chalet on the shores of Lake Chiemsee, furnished to a high standard—"with perfect taste," noted Sainto. They had a piano, horses, and they could go sailing on the immense lake. The chalet belonged to the brother-in-law of Hermann Goering, the commander of the Nazi Air Force, now being held in an Allied prison.

Moments like these were so rare, incongruous given the dystopian world they'd traversed. July came, with more unexpected relief. The girls who had brought some men to Strasbourg stopped off at Lake Constance, and the ones who had gone to Salzburg for valves joined them there for what would turn out to be their last "normal" moments for a long time to come. "The valves are fed up," Sainto wrote. "We aren't. Our friendship keeps growing. The joy we see in the eyes of the men we transport in these ambulances is the best reward of all. What memories, what adventures!" Miche and Petit Bob had brought back new valves from Salzburg, and while the engines were being repaired, there was a bit more time to relax. It was the eve of July 14, the French national holiday. On the island of Reichenau, on Lake Constance, they allowed themselves a bath. The weather was beautiful and calm, and the upheaval that was still shaking Europe seemed far away. A moment of grace before setting off again, this time to their most grueling mission.

At the lakeside, they had a chance to share their memories, and what stood out was their brief time in Czechoslovakia, which was their first experience of the Russian zone. It left its mark on them, especially the sight of the Red Army and its conditions. "It was like an engraving from Napoleon's time, troika, horses, straw," Sainto wrote. The wounded were lying on it, and the roads were slippery, covered with manure several centimeters thick.

Back in the lakeside town of Constance, the buildings were decked out in blue, white, and red, in honor of the French national holiday. After a theatrical performance, a grand dinner for five hundred guests was held. Some American aviators offered them what would be the first flight of their lives. "They gave us a great display of acrobatics," noted Sainto. "I came back thrilled, while others were sick as hell."

How good it was to experience this moment of comradery and pleasure, like a little soap bubble, a moment of rejoicing, but it wouldn't last long.

The Blue Squadron awaited further orders, until, finally, a phone call settled everything. There had been negotiations with the Russians, which had opened the door for the Squadron to go to Warsaw, their next destination, driving the ambulances across the German-Polish border. They were keeping their fingers crossed that they would be able to rescue the French nationals who, they've been told, were there, and in desperate need.

Still, there was a question of some leave time for the overworked crews. Sainto asked for two or three days' leave, "so we can embrace our families and get some warm clothes."

"It's not a good idea," says Guillot.

"Why?"

"Because if you tell your family that you're going to the Russian zone, they're bound to object. Think about it."

In the end, they stayed, all of them. Tschupp spent time with what the girls called "her Canadian," a soldier she'd met, and they wondered if she was going to stay behind. "You have to make the most of every moment," said Sainto. "She's a wonderful girl. Twenty-nine years old; she's got a lot of spirit and a serenity that never deserts her. If she doesn't come, I'll be sorry." There was a moment of suspense as they waited to learn what Tschupp would do. Will she go or stay? In the end, she went, like the others.

Finally, on July 23, they set off for Poland. They were having a bout of the blues; the mood was dark after their lakeside respite. "It's the

Figure 10.3 Violette Guillot in a Red Cross jeep. "Sainto" writes of her, "We were assigned to Mobile Group number one, whose chief was Guillot. She had a masculine allure, short hair pulled back, an intimidating air but sometimes with an extraordinary smile; she would turn out to have a heart of gold and was a magnificent chief."

unknown," Sainto wrote in her diary by way of explanation. "Yesterday we left Augsburg loaded down with Czechs"—another transport of Czech prisoners. There were several such transports, and if this one left from Augsburg, they would have driven northeast across the Czech border to Pilsen, and then, to get to Poland, the 83 kilometers through the countryside to Prague. "The trip went very well. The countryside was delightful. At first, it was vast fields of wheat. Then a pretty little town with delightful houses of all colors. We crossed the Danube at Deggendorf, where the river is wide but horribly dirty. Hordes of people were bathing everywhere there was some water. Ah, those lucky mortals! How we would have loved to take a dip with them! In the end, dead tired and quarrelsome, we slept at the Communist Party quarters. The next day, we went to the cinema and then on the way back, we all felt blue. We laughed; we talked nonsense. How far we were from those we love and who love us. . . . It's wonderful to be a volunteer, but that doesn't stop you from seeing things the way they are."

On July 26, the little troop set off again, at half past three in the morning, with six hundred kilometers to go. The five ambulances were running well. But the fuel on the road was of poor quality, and the carburetors got clogged. The squadron crossed Prague. A last look at the city for Sainto, who, by her own admission, had left a piece of her heart behind.

One stop followed another. The engine had to be cleaned, the fuel lines unclogged, a tire changed. The girls had lunch on the grass, then set off again. Late in the evening, they arrived at the border. To the left was Jelenia Góra, the Green Mountain. To the right, the road to Krakow and Auschwitz. There was a bridge over the Olga River. The five ambulances stopped. Never would any of them forget this passage across the Czech-Polish frontier. A Russian officer, who ought to have respected their right of passage, immediately demanded to see them, all of them. He ordered them to descend from their ambulances, then, lined up, they waited a long time as the man examined them, coming close, looking at each of them, their faces seeming to be an object of particular attention. Finally, they heard an order given to their leader, Ducroquet, that made them tremble, an order to bring him one of them that night—"whichever one you want," he adds.

It was the arrival of two officers, a Russian and a French officer, that would save the situation. They appeared by car, a moving sight, this meeting between two Allied combatants. "It all seems so simple," noted Sainto. At seven o'clock in the evening, the Blue Squadron crossed the border. This was the zone forbidden by the Soviet authorities to anyone without special permission. The road was potholed; crumbling slag heaps lined the horizon; chimneys belched dirty smoke. They reached Katowice, at last, where they were given a warm greeting, beginning with cherry soup, vodka, bread, and the ultimate luxury—butter.

Russian women directed traffic; horses pulled poor carts. They'd had an escort since crossing the border, and he explained the rules under which they would be working. They were draconian. Every activity, every movement, must be reported to the occupying authorities, and to no one else. Every prisoner, every wounded person, must be identified. Every thought, every opinion, must be recorded. In short, Sainto noted,

Figure 10.4 All along its route, the Blue Squadron witnessed the wounds of war: the rusted barbed wire, the carcasses of wrecked trucks, collapsed bridges covered by logs, as in this photograph. Sainto writes, "As the ambulance advanced, the logs bunched together in a mound. We had to reset them and push. . . . It was exhausting at times."

"Everything now is forbidden. Forbidden to say where we're going. Time is forbidden to go by. It's forbidden almost to think."

Welcome to liberated Poland.

In two days, the Blue Squadron would be in Warsaw. Madeleine eagerly awaited them.

Chapter 11

"WE'D DIE FOR PAULIAC"

(July 27, 1945)

My aunt, a slender young woman with wavy brown hair, was at Warsaw's French Hospital, in the Praga suburb of Warsaw, the only part of Poland's capital with intact buildings. The stone house was flanked by an outside staircase, where she was standing. She had come out for a breath of fresh air, to escape the confined atmosphere of the treatment rooms. Her pale eyes scanned the street, mechanically. Later today, or tomorrow at the latest, she was expecting the group of ambulance drivers and nurses to arrive and to lend her a hand. Madeleine had fought to receive this help, as she did for every improvement in the treatment of wounded French citizens.

Initially, she'd had only one room in the building that housed the Polish Red Cross dispensary. Opening the hospital marked a big improvement, but so much remained to be done.

Just as she was about to climb back up the stairs, she spotted a car at the end of the street, and since cars were rare enough in this martyred country, she stayed there and watched, hoping—and then, with gladness in her heart, she saw that it wasn't just one car but a convoy of five bulky Austin ambulances making their way toward her. Yes! It was them! The nurses and ambulance drivers of the Blue Squadron had finally arrived in Warsaw, and Madeleine felt like one of those medieval damsels in a castle, rescued at last.

To get to Warsaw, the eleven young women had crossed the ruins of Europe, which was still in the grip of devastating madness. Germany, Czechoslovakia, and Poland were ravaged, and the young women had

Figure 11.1   View of the French Hospital in Warsaw, where so many lives were saved. Created largely by Madeleine and her colleague Charles Liber, its mission was to rescue French nationals trapped in Poland, but they were unable to ignore the many Polish women and children who came to them for help. The author found the building still intact on a visit to Warsaw in 2016.

witnessed incredible scenes, the aftermaths of massacres and other horrors coming after five years of war, and those discoveries had forged their determination even as it had changed their view of the world.

"Come in," Madeleine said as the squadron disembarked from their bulky jeeps. One by one, they met the doctor, led, most likely, by Guillot, their leader. Madeleine would soon learn that she'd been the head of a mobile medical unit since at least January, already part of a team with Tschupp and Stiffler. From a Protestant family, her brother was a ranking officer in the Salvation Army in Britain, so she seemed to have had a duty to public service inscribed in her genes. She'd met Micheline Reveron during the liberation of Marseilles in August 1944, and the two of them had been inseparable since then. The others—Sainto, Tschupp, Braye, Pagès, and the rest—presented themselves to Dr. Pauliac—who'd already been in Warsaw for three months—with a sense of seriousness, a willed energy, about what lay ahead.

"We'll have dinner," Madeleine told them. "We've recovered some American rations, you'll see!" A few slices of corned beef, a little horseradish, industrial sausage, and black bread "like the devil's soul" were enough to put smiles on the faces of the young women, already used to hardship.

What struck them at first was the great gentleness of Madeleine's face, framed by her long, wavy chestnut hair. But her blue eyes showed the fierceness the squadron members would come to know well as the rescue mission unfolded. She had done a lot already to prepare the ground, made some contacts, created the French Hospital, traveled to Gdansk, and begun, with the help of Liber and the others, to look for men from France lost on the fringes of the areas controlled by the Red Army. Now, with reinforcements, the work could go on at a much higher scale. But the task ahead was complicated and dangerous. Much had happened in the time between Madeleine's and the Blue Squadron's arrival in Warsaw. Most important and obviously, Germany had surrendered, and the war had ended in Europe. Russian troops, having fought their way across Poland, were now effectively an occupying force, and a ruthless one, there to carry out the Russian leader Joseph Stalin's policy to establish a communist government in Poland that would be subservient to Moscow. Madeleine's mission, now reinforced by the arrival of the Blue Squadron, was to organize the repatriation of wounded compatriots who had somehow gotten lost behind the Oder-Neisse line, the newly established border between Germany and Poland and the unofficial point marking the end of the Soviet zone of influence. And they had very little time to accomplish the task, since at that very moment, Soviet control was being consolidated; what later came to be called the Iron Curtain was making its swift descent, cutting Poland off from the West.

In February 1945, as noted earlier, Stalin, Roosevelt, and Churchill met in the Crimean city of Yalta. At that time, they were still more or less cordially discussing arrangements after the anticipated defeat of Germany and Japan. The American and British had agreed that pro-Russian communists would be included in the provisional Polish government, but also that free and fair elections would be held there once the war was over. But in reality, by the time of Germany's surrender on May 8, the Soviet Red Army completely controlled Poland, and Moscow was maneuvering to install its puppet pro-communist Polish government there. The Soviets would dominate Poland for the next forty-five years, refusing to hold the promised elections. And despite their repatriation agreement with the French government, they had no intention of giving carte blanche to a group of French humanitarians to rescue their French compatriots and return them to France.

Despite the considerable hurdles, soon after their arrival, the women of the Blue Squadron got to work. The very day they were received by Madeleine, they called at the French Embassy across the street from the French Hospital. It was there, on a windswept terrace on the top floor, where the eleven new arrivals spent a stormy first night before moving into a house that had been repainted by volunteers and furnished with salvaged materials. There was no running water, no electricity. The nearby river, the Vistula, was their water supply, despite the corpses still floating on its surface. Hospital stretchers would have to serve as beds for a while. But this band of sisters had already been hardened by their weeks on the road. They'd witnessed Dachau and Buchenwald; they'd driven all night, slept in their ambulances, gotten their hands dirty cleaning air filters and carburetors; men had died in their arms. But they had also sung the Marseillaise in exhilaration as they transported French former prisoners across the Rhine and back into their beloved France. These spirited young women were primed for what was to come.

After dinner, the young women headed for their makeshift work-place. There was a large terrace at the top of the hospital overlooking the Vistula River. As a tremendous thunderstorm erupted, they contemplated the destroyed city illuminated by lightning, and what they saw was ruins, an apocalyptic landscape. Everything had been destroyed in Warsaw; everything needed to be redone.

And so, it was the start of an incredible sisterhood, the beginning of a epic endeavor for these women. Madeleine Pauliac was the first to have ventured into the most hostile territory, controlled by a violent army sure of its right to plunder, kill, and rape, to make someone else pay for the years of war and deprivation suffered by Russia. As we shall see, Madeleine was up to the challenge. She would be a tutelary figure for the women of the Blue Squadron, truly a beacon in the night, a friend, and, in the end, an irreplaceable loss. All the women were exemplary; all had tremendous strength, but Madeleine had an aura about her that encouraged the others to follow her, to trust her, to rely on her.

And a year later, that aura was frozen by her brutal and premature death, in the Poland she wanted to help at all costs. It was an aura whose history is marked by the men and women she saved, by the children whose destinies she made possible. The children whose stories she entrusted to my mother, who, in turn, passed them on to me. These

Figure 11.2 Eight of "the Blues" standing on the cement staircase leading to the French Hospital in Warsaw. They are, from top to bottom: Madeleine Pauliac, Charlotte Pagés, Violette Guillot, Aline Tschupp, Jeanine Robert ("Petit Bob"), Élizabeth Blaise, Cécile Stiffler, Jacqueline Heiniger, and Simone Saint-Olive ("Sainto"). Micheline Reveron is missing because she's taking the picture. Simone Bray and Francoise Lagrange weren't present at the time.

children are with me as I write these lines, like little fireflies guiding my steps.

Who were they?

Maybe we'll find out one day.

The Abbé Beilliard said mass. Released in Germany, he, too, preferred to stay and continue his priesthood, rather than return home to Picardy in the north of France. He usually wore an American parka and a khaki shirt. But today, in his makeshift surplice, found in a church that had been vandalized by the Soviets, he paid homage to God and asked for the remission of sins, then concluded, in front of the improvised altar set up in the dispensary: "*Ite, missa est*"—Go, the mass is ended. He gave the last blessing, and two nuns in the background crossed themselves. The abbot closed his missal, then moved to a chair that served as the sacristy. In his liturgical vestments, he looked very serious, but, in fact, he was a jovial man with an irrepressible zest for life. He knew how to make the sort of jokes that put everyone at ease.

Madeleine approached him. She was no longer a believer herself, but she respected other people's faith and commitments, especially of men like the Abbé Beilliard, entirely devoted to his fellow man. Sainto followed her, along with the rest of the team.

"Monsieur l'abbé, I'd like to introduce you to the Blue Squadron," Madeleine said. "They've just arrived from France."

After their long drive through a desolate landscape, the young women were comforted to find warmth and friendship. They were moved by the welcome they received from "the doctor Pauliac," as they'd called her. It was as if they'd known each other all their lives. The bonds forged along the way in Germany among the girls in the ambulance teams were broad and deep. But there was room for all people of goodwill, and Madeleine Pauliac was immediately adopted.

Sainto wrote in her diary, "The hospital is Pauliac's work. We have a friendship that warms us." Later, she added, "We'd die for Pauliac. She is our driving force, full of affection."

This immediate closeness, this understanding from the very first days, was recounted to me by Sainto herself, and confirmed by the testimonials that were made by other members of the Squadron at Madeleine's funeral. "She was extraordinary—everyone said so," read one comment. I devoted a lot of thought to understanding why. Was it due to circumstances? We know adversity can bring people together. Or was it their personalities? Most fundamentally, these young women, despite their social differences, had been educated so that they shared a basic need—to be useful, to help, to do "what they could," a need that was on everyone's lips and in everyone's letters. They were driven by this shared ideal, this shared goal. And there was another common reaction: they were always modest when it came to discussing what they did, saying that they were "only doing their duty." In his tribute at Madeleine's funeral mass, Abbé Beilliard spoke of her "disdainful" response when her work was praised.

After meeting Abbé Beilliard, the girls of the Squadron went into the city with Captain Birckel. But what city? Warsaw was no longer a city; it was a gigantic magma. In the cleared streets, a few children played with makeshift toys: arrows carved from branches, feathers found who knows where, cowboy hats cut from newspapers. The Soviet army was camped everywhere. Birckel explained to the girls how the town had been methodically destroyed by the Germans, while Soviet troops bivouacked just a few kilometers away on the other side of the Vistula, their weapons at their feet.

Only one palace and two churches had survived the fire and bombardment. But everything else—apartment blocks, schools, museums, universities, theaters, hospitals, power stations, railway stations, banks, factories—was destroyed. Hitler's plan had been to wipe Warsaw off the map.

"It's all so sad, so terribly sad," a pale Petit Bob says. "It's a cemetery of men and stones here."

On a crossroads in the center of town, loudspeakers had been set up, blaring out names: Novak, Milena, Schreiber, Levy, Bitkovicz, Choro, Kazimierz—an endless litany. Parents were looking for their children, children were looking for their parents, scattered families wanting to reunite. It was heartbreaking. It was the first-year anniversary of the Warsaw Uprising, a bitter birthday.

On their return from their excursion into the heart of darkness, the Blue Squadron received their next mission orders from Madeleine. Tschupp and Guillot were ordered to a camp in the south. The others would take care of the long line of women in front of the hospital. There were typhus patients, victims of terrible burns, unrecognizable faces, bruised or totally ravaged. Hunger, above all, marked their bodies. Supplies were nonexistent; they'd been seized by the Russians.

Every day, Madeleine performed surgical operations. The gloomy procession never stopped. Men presented wounds that had been hastily stitched up and had to be reopened, traumas that had never been treated, epidemic diseases. The conditions for intervention were minimal. New, previously unknown wounds appeared. Phosphorus-charred skin, penetrating funnel wounds caused by flat-tipped bullets, sexual lesions caused by torture inflicted by barbaric SS men. Madeleine performed ligations and laparotomies and tried to bring the victims out of their state of shock.

And how to talk to the children? In their eyes, fear mingled with incomprehension. For the youngest, war and misfortune were all they'd ever known, and yet they knew that pain and sadness were not normal. They knew instinctively that a better world was possible. Just as when she chose to work at the Hôpital des Enfants-Malades in Paris,

Madeleine knew why she was there. To offer them a better world, to the best of her ability.

Given her childhood, which I know about from my mother's memories, Madeleine must have been acutely aware of what adults could do for children, and what they could do to them. The tug-of-war between her mother and grandmother, and the differences in character between them, very quickly taught the two sisters a certain form of relativity—that nobody was completely right—but it also opened their eyes to the responsibility of adults toward children. One could not just say anything or do just anything. The slightest word, the slightest encouragement, had effects that "grown-ups" didn't always appreciate. The adults who showed the most respect for children were those who remembered their own childhoods.

And what if it was also a matter of small symbols? In this dark world, Sainto decided to react. With Petit Bob, she went to the little market not far from the hospital to buy flowers. A few touches of color brightened up the rooms.

"This will please Stiffler," said Petit Bob. "She's in bed this morning."

"What's wrong with her?" Madeleine asked.

"An attack of acute gastroenteritis, she has a fever of 39.5 Centigrade."

Madeleine thought for a second. "I've got some opium left. I'll get it."

The Blue Squadron set to work with a relentlessness and determination that struck Madeleine as extraordinary. Nothing deterred them. "On returning from a mission," Madeleine wrote in a report, "thankless tasks await the teams. Given how shorthanded we are, all the ambulance drivers have to scrub the hospital's floors and windows, carry out the chore of getting water, clean up patients as they arrive, day and night, on the convoys coming from Russia, which bring in men in an appalling state."

It's more than a mission; it's almost a priesthood.

For the French, led by Roger Garreau, understanding the workings of the new state could sometimes be a headache. Garreau had just presented his credentials to Polish president Boleslaw Bierut, the doctrinaire communist president of the Polish National Council, which led the country's provisional government, though the ultimate political power was unquestionably in Moscow. The organization of the Polish Workers' Party was mysterious. The Central Committee was comprised of thirty-three members, along with the Politburo and the ministers, but who was at the top of the hierarchy—Boleslaw Bierut, Wladislaw Gomulka, or Jakub Berman? And what was the role of Roman Zambrowski, an obscure figure allied with Hilary Minc, the minister of industry? The new power, supported by Moscow, multiplied its functions. Directors, prefects, commissioners, regional leaders, organizers, advisors—all were communists. The militia was commanded by officers from the NKVD, the Soviet spy agency, predecessor to the KGB. German property was confiscated, land collectivized.

In an anonymous report at the end of June, a writer noted that the chief characteristic of the Polish government was "almost complete inefficiency." He emphasized the absolute lack of independence of the authorities, whose "decisions are subject to ratification by Russian commissioners" whose policies are formed without regard for the country's needs. There were Russian commissions at every level of the administrative hierarchy. Nothing could be obtained or accomplished without their consent. The writer went on to note that the destruction of all means of communication and travel made things even more complicated.

The Polish Church, at least in outward appearance, was preserved. "Sincere Catholics will work hand in hand with the authorities," said Cardinal Hlond, soon to be named Archbishop of Warsaw, and a complicated figure who spent the war years in Gestapo custody and later was a harsh critic of the communist regime.

But churches were being burned.

The Potsdam Conference, concluded on August 2, 1945, fixed the zones of occupation among the Russians, the Americans, the British, and the French, and affirmed that the former eastern territories of Germany would be given to Poland. Soon, eleven million Germans would hit the road, leaving their farms and homes in what was now Polish territory and migrating west across the new German border.

In Poland, where French property had already been nationalized, French influence was diminishing. From Moscow, General Catroux sent a report on relations with the USSR, with clear conclusions: "It is pointless to pursue a cooperative effort to which the Soviet government does not respond. France should seek support elsewhere than in Moscow."

General de Gaulle's idea, then, was to suggest the formation of a common policy, a grouping of the powers of Western Europe, an idea publicly expressed in a statement to the *Times* in Paris, as revealed in the headline, "De Gaulle Vows to Create 'a Western Bloc.'"

Stalin was furious. He interpreted these wishes as an "attempt to sabotage" peace. The USSR, the homeland of socialism, felt undeniably threatened. Relations between France and the USSR deteriorated.

Under the circumstances, Madeleine knew that the mission's days were numbered and that the repatriation team had to act tirelessly, while it was still possible. The French presence in Poland was still tolerated, barely, but for how much longer?

Two months earlier, she had been visited by two nuns who had attended a mass with Abbé Beilliard. They were in a desperate condition. God had clearly forgotten them, and yet they maintained their faith. Their headdresses were shabby, their tunics wrinkled. The eldest wore a large rosary on her belt. Their convent, they told Madeleine, was in the nearby forest, some thirty kilometers away. In their vow of solitude, they were committed to silence, meditation, and withdrawal from the world. Yet here they were, crying out for help.

Were they hurt? No. Sick? Some were. Undernourished? Certainly.

Madeleine suggested contacting the Polish Red Cross.

This was out of the question, the nuns replied.

"Come and see us," the older woman insisted.

"I'll bring one of the hospital doctors."

"No, please come alone. It's a favor we ask of you. And don't mention this to anyone."

Madeleine took off her medical coat, rinsed her hands, and asked where the monastery was. Abbé Beilliard, she thought, would be a good advisor on this matter, but he was away. Never mind, she decided to go alone with these nuns, who reminded her of the ones she had met in Danzig earlier.

As they approached the high walls of the convent, after parking the Red Cross car, Madeleine looked at the headdress of the nun in front of her. During the journey, the two women prayed in silence. Now they hurried off, as if afraid of something. Madeleine shivered in the damp night.

The wooden door opened. Madeleine would never forget what she discovered behind it.

For my part, I still remember my mother's emotions as if it were yesterday as she described what her sister found in that desecrated convent in the Polish woods. She had kept it all to herself for so long, feeling bound not to let anything slip. And then the years passed, conditions changed, children grew up, and mothers died. One day, my mother decided it was time to tell what she knew, and in bits and pieces, she related the secret that Madeleine had discovered that night when she followed two Polish nuns into the forest.

Chapter 12

ESCAPES

(August–September 1945)

Thanks to information gleaned from correspondents in the prison camps or from those who managed to reach the French Hospital on their own, the repatriation team continued to receive information on the whereabouts of French nationals who needed to be rescued. The Blue Squadron quickly made themselves an integral part of the mission, working closely with Madeleine and the others on the French team. "Act quickly, act discreetly" were the watchwords of the day.

Twice a week, a plane left Le Bourget Airport in Paris to pick up the men to be repatriated. André Ribeiro in a crew with Pruneau, Thual, and Ménager, then by Gey and Quesnel (their first names are lost to history), took turns making these flights, which were not easy. From Le Bourget, they had to make a stop in Fassberg, in the British occupation zone of northern Germany, where there was a Royal Air Force base. That was where they refueled, because Warsaw, of course, had no refueling facilities. Then it was on to Berlin via the "central corridor," an airspace protected for the Western powers. They had to fly almost at ground level, which was made possible by the low-altitude terrain, because the Russians didn't provide radio navigation. They left Le Bourget on Monday, arrived in Warsaw on Tuesday, and on Wednesday they embarked on the reverse route. Ribeiro, in a testimony written after the war, noted that the men being repatriated were brought to the Warsaw airfield "by a Red Cross team consisting of a dozen or so nurses and ambulance drivers who have roamed all the roads of Poland and Danzig." After a certain time, "we came to sympathize with some of them, and to say that on the steps of the hospital I didn't kiss a certain Jacqueline, lively, pink and fresh as a daisy, would be false," Ribeiro wrote, describing a nascent love story taking place amid the chaos, "but it didn't go farther than that."

One day, not long after the Blue Squadron had gotten to work, Sainto told Madeleine that some wounded Frenchmen had just arrived on their own. They'd walked, then climbed onto carts, hidden in tarpaulin-covered trucks. They were exhausted and needed urgent attention, especially as these men had escaped from the Soviet hospital in Bialystok.

It was Ducroquet who received them and who immediately gauged the danger they faced. Because the Russians had refused to release them, the men had covered over two hundred kilometers from Bialystok to make it to Warsaw, arriving in a state of great weakness. They had no papers, and if the Ivans were to get wind of them, the diplomatic situation would have become untenable. There had been formal protests issued to the American Embassy, because Bliss Lane, the US ambassador, had issued passes to the West and visas to the United States. It was a ticklish matter for the Soviets, who didn't like it when their prey was snuck away from them. The era of the Cold War had unquestionably begun. In his memoirs, Bliss Lane revealed the secret agreement struck between the Lublin government and Moscow, under which the Soviets had the right to deport, on the spot, anyone considered "dangerous to the Red Army": other words, anyone for any reason.

The Blue Squadron went into battle mode. The boys who had arrived from Bialystok were absolutely certain that there were other compatriots laid up in the Russian hospital who would be deported to the Urals in the next few days. There, they would be out of reach. The trouble was, Bialystok was close to the Soviet border, and the road, which passed through Ostrów, Mazowiecka, and Zambrów, was clogged with Red Army vehicles. Brutally colonized by the Nazis during the war, Bialystok underwent a succession of terrible massacres, most notably in the ghetto in August 1943, from which tens of thousands of Jews were departed to Majdanek and Treblinka. For the Russians, it was a strategic crossing point. All supplies for troops in Poland and Germany passed through here. The road from Warsaw to Bialystok continued on into the USSR, about two hundred miles away. Once brought across

the border into Soviet Russia, the Frenchmen, now essentially imprisoned in the Bialystok hospital, would have been beyond reach.

Madeleine, Sainto, Petit Bob, and the other girls split up in two
ambulances, with Birckel, their interpreter, in one. They left right away,
while Ducroquet remained in Warsaw. The road was hard, and the
urgency of the task ahead was felt by everyone. The ambulances passed
Russian trucks loaded with tired soldiers, American jeeps supplied to the
Soviets as part of the US war effort, and Polish carts between the heavy
vehicles, their horses panting. Burned-out tanks lay in the ditch, and all
the trees along the road were torn to shreds. The fighting here had been
very violent. On this flat land, which offered no shelter, the progress of
the armies had been paid for at a high price. Far and wide, mass graves
bore witness to the barbarity that had taken place. Soon, Madeleine
mused, nature would reclaim its rights. Bones would become dust,
victims and executioners would turn to earth, trees would grow back,
and everything would return to the way it had been. Memory would
fade. No one would know that this landscape had been soaked in blood,
that history had impregnated every leaf, every plant, every flower, with
an immense sadness. From the ambulance, there were fields of poppies
stretching as far as the eye could see, like those in the famous song sung
by the Polish soldiers who captured the German stronghold on Monte
Cassino in Italy in May 1944. It was a sea of red rippling in the wind
across the infinite plain. For Madeleine, the sight was reminiscent of the
streets of Villeneuve-sur-Lot, covered by red tomato juice when the
Pauliac cannery used to deliver tons of the fruit. Red wasn't always an
ugly color.

In Zambrów, a stele dating from the town's incorporation into
Lithuania informed the team that the town had been bombed by the
Germans in April 1915. It was a grim reminder of an earlier barbarity, a
particularly painful thought for Madeleine, whose father, Roger Pauliac,
had had to suffer the consequences of it. Men never remember anything.
History is a stutterer.

The Bialystok hospital was at the end of a straight street that had
changed names many times, reflecting the ebb and flow of conquerors. It
used to be Friedrichstrasse, then Hitlerstrasse, and it would soon become
Ulica Stalina, but for the moment, it bore no sign. The city lay on a flat
surface, with no hills, no heights—everything was level. The result was

a strange feeling of monotony, which induced a kind of lethargy. But you had to do everything fast there, otherwise you would get bogged down in this immensity, this immobility. It was like a poison that emanated from the land itself. If you didn't move, you were mummified. Chekhov sensed this, this gravity that resembled death. To act, to act quickly, was the remedy, the only remedy.

Madeleine was determined to fight. Accompanied by Sainto and Petit Bob, she presented herself to the officer at the entrance. Birckel translated.

"We are the French mission. We've come to pick up French patients."

"Which French patients? Papers!"

"French people being treated in this hospital. Here are our papers."

"There are no French here. Only Poles and Russians."

"We've had reports of French people."

"Who's 'we'? There have never been any French people here. They're in Paris."

"Can we look?"

"Not possible."

"I insist."

"Not possible. Not possible."

"Can we see the head doctor?"

"No."

"What about our embassy?"

"Do as you please. I've got better things to do than listen to you."

The Russian turned on his heel and left. Madeleine was revolted; Petit Bob foamed at the mouth. The other girls waited in the ambulances. Night fell. They had to find a place to sleep. Guillot discovered a barn still standing, cluttered with rusty scrap metal. The heat of the day began to wane, but the earth was still soaked with sunshine.

Madeleine was determined not to give up. She didn't accept failure. The practice of medicine had taught her that you had to fight to the last extremity. In war, too. The Liberation was proof to her that her resistance activities had been justified. She drew inspiration from them. You must try every strategy, except procrastination.

Courage? Recklessness? The audacity of youth? This episode is one of those that makes me wonder what I, in their situation, would have been able to do. Would I have been able to forget the risks, or my fear? Would I have admitted defeat and gone back the way I came? Or would I, like them, have given it my all? These are dizzying questions, to which, needless to say, no answers can be given in peacetime.

The next day, everyone was back at the hospital. The Russian officer had been replaced by a Polish senior doctor, who evidently didn't want to help the French team for fear of angering the Russians. But Madeleine, who had made a plan, had given everyone a role to play. While Birckel conferred with the head doctor, Tschupp and Miche slipped into the administration office to go through the registers and get the hospital admissions forms. Madeleine, with the rest of the team, walked briskly around the building, entering through the back door. Along the two floors of wards, the girls moved quickly, opening each door and shouting.

"Are there any French people? French people?"

"Here!"

"This way, Sainto!"

In a few beds at the end of the room lay eight Frenchmen, wounded in various ways. One of them had a broken leg. Madeleine asked, "Any others?"

"No. Just us," replied a small, swarthy man, with the accent of the Midi.

"Right, then. Here's what we're going to do."

As she quickly explained the procedure, the eight men sat up, some with difficulty, on their beds. One was looking for his shoes, the other for his bandages. Suddenly, someone started to sing in a low voice. Two or three voices joined in, but softly, so as not to warn the Russians. A minute later, the eight men, standing, leaning on each other, were ready. They sang, in, mezzo voce, *"Allons enfants de la Patrie!"* It was the Marseillaise.

> Arise, children of the fatherland,
> The day of glory has come.
> Against us, the bloody flag of tyranny
> Is raised. The bloody flag is raised.

Madeleine looked at the haggard faces of the men, their clasped hands, their bent silhouettes. These men were suffering, but the joy of being with Frenchwomen drove them on. France had come to fetch them from the depths of the East. Freedom was at hand. Tears flowed, eyes shone, and despite the suffering, smiles blossomed.

Madeleine was overwhelmed.

But there was no time to waste. In two minutes, the operation was launched under Madeleine's command, and it was like a raid. The able-bodied quickly headed for the back door, while the disabled were helped by the women. The two ambulances, already parked at the site, filled up. The doors closed, and the first vehicle started up. As soon as he heard the engines, Birckel said he had forgotten something and left the head doctor there. Tschupp and Miche put down the hospital records and got going quickly, escaping in the second ambulance. The Russians, taken by surprise, started yelling. Shots were heard. One of the Russian guards rushed over, and with Petit Bob at the wheel, the door opened on Birckel's side. The Russian hung on, climbed onto the running board. Then, suddenly, he let go and rolled into the dust.

There was no stopping now. The drivers put their feet to the floor, taking a different route than before. It was impossible to keep going fast, however. In some sections, the ambulances had to move at a snail's pace. But they got to Warsaw at the end of the day, and instead of going to the hospital, Madeleine decided to head straight for the airfield. The Dakota that flew to Paris twice a week was there. Just before boarding, one of the Frenchmen said thank you.

"If you hadn't kidnapped us, we'd have ended up like the others."

"What do you mean by 'the others'?"

"We would have been shipped East, and there would have been no way back. But now, if all goes well, I'll be at Batignolles in two days, drinking a little white wine."

"I hope you do. Have a nice trip!"

The women waved their scarves as the Dakota took off. André Ribeiro, the pilot, waved his hand. Jacqueline Heiniger watched for a long time as the aircraft pulled away. The Dakota would be back. So would André. Jacqueline would wait.

Petit Bob burst out laughing. "We really had them going, didn't we?"

Figure 12.1 Wounded men being put on the weekly flight from Warsaw to Paris.

But that allusion to "the others" hung like a dark cloud over the celebration.

A few days later, two Frenchmen arrived at the hospital, part of a convoy of convalescents bound for the USSR. Communist Party members, they fought with the International Brigades in Barcelona during the Spanish Civil War, in the Henri-Barbusse battalion, and then came under the command of "General Kléber," the pseudonym of a Hungarian Red Army volunteer whom they followed on his return to Moscow. But they were wounded and got stuck in Poland, and now, being taken to the USSR, they jumped off the train.

Other French people were on the carriages, they told Madeleine.

She immediately climbed into an ambulance, direction: Kaluszyn station, not far from Warsaw and the next stop on the rail line. But by the time she got there, the train had already left. The next station, Jagodne, was just around the corner. She set off again, but night fell, and the road darkened. It was too late. What would become of these Frenchmen? No one knew.

From time to time, on television, I'd see reports about French people who'd found themselves in the depths of the USSR, now the Russian Federation. I wasn't yet as familiar with the subject as I am now,

Figure 12.2   A group of the nurses waving goodbye as the weekly flight to Le Bourget Airport in Paris takes off from the Warsaw airfield, carrying some of the injured and sick Frenchmen rescued by the Blue Squadron.

but the fate of the men like the ones who came so close to Madeleine but were lost in the turmoil of events had already made a deep impression on me. I remember watching an elderly man speaking in French as part of a televised report from Russia. This would have been half a century after Madeleine's time in Poland. He was one of those—and there were many of them—who had not been repatriated years before, and he'd lived miserably in Russia ever since, and probably would for the rest of his life.

The pace of the sorties made by the team quickened. Equipped with safe-conduct passes, the girls of the Blue Squadron crisscrossed the region, under Madeleine's precise orders. One of the most serious problems was that patients were often moved from hospital to hospital, some six times in one month, so that the repatriation team would hear about a French group at one location, but by the time they got there, the men were gone. Then, when they got back to Warsaw, they would learn that the men they'd been searching for had been brought back to the earlier place.

Still, the hospital in Warsaw expanded. General Catroux's wife, Marguerite, managed to secure some fifty beds. Now there were eleven military officers; three doctors, including Madeleine; some fifteen nurses; seven ambulances; three trucks; and three cars. Six train wagons had brought medical supplies from Moscow. From France, the first mission from SIPEG—the French acronym for Interministerial Service for Protection against the Events of War—arrived. It was a hospital train, under the direction of Doctor-Captain Denise Bourgeois, bringing clothing, food, medicine, and petrol. It was a harrowing weeklong journey from the Gare du Nord in Paris to the Grochow marshaling yard in Praga. Other SIPEG trains followed, still under the command of Dr. Bourgeois. Mail, too, arrived more regularly. Madeleine read letters from her sister, Anne-Marie, and from her mother. Immediately, a wave of happiness swept over her, and the dreariness of the day faded away.

Information was flowing in. It was said that there was a large concentration of French prisoners at Tambov, in Soviet territory, five hundred kilometers south of Moscow.

They were mainly Alsatians and people from the Moselle region of eastern France. When the French authorities asked for them, the Russians generously offered to shoot them, to spare the Westerners the unpleasant task of coming to retrieve them. But this was not so strange, since all these men had been seized wearing German uniforms, whether because they were taken prisoner and were forced to fight for Germany, or whether they volunteered to do so. The Russians, obligingly, were ready to do the dirty work.

One of the mission's doctors, a Commandant Nouaille (his first name does not appear in the archives), reported that two thousand Frenchmen were on their way west from Tambov, and a train had arrived at Lukow station, three hours away, and its route would take it to the town of Radom, south of Warsaw. The task was to intercept it. Madeleine embarked for Radom with the women of the Blue Squadron and several trucks. Unfortunately, the train had already left for Lodz, though about forty Frenchmen got off the train and were found on the platform.

Sainto noted in her diary, "I have confidence in Major N. . . . He's just graduated from Polytechnique. Unfortunately, he's fallen in love with me. But he's old, at least thirty!"

Major Nouaille died in active service three months later, in the village of Ban Me Thuot in Vietnam, during France's doomed effort to maintain its colonial empire in Southeast Asia.

In this burned-out world, Madeleine received an invitation, which she passed on to the women of the Blue Squadron. On September 4, in Warsaw, there would be a piano recital, with Henryk Sztompka at the keyboard. The profits would go to rebuilding Warsaw's Holy Cross Church, where the event would take place. It would be the first public concert in liberated Poland. By evening, the emotion was palpable. A printed program was distributed to the audience, the entire Allied community, dressed up to attend the event. Uniforms had been ironed, everyone dressed as if it was before the war, when concerts were the highlight of social and cultural life. It was a veritable rebirth of "normal" life, the expression of an infinitely comforting humanity. It is sometimes difficult to imagine the extent to which art nourishes the soul, but it does. I found the program in the papers passed down to me by my mother, and it was Sainto who told me how it unfolded and what it meant. Seventy years later, her emotion was evident in every word.

Sztompka began with Sonata No. 2, Op. 35 by Chopin on the composer's piano, and as he played, a respectful silence settled on the crowd. After the "Funeral March," also by Chopin, it seemed to everyone that soft light penetrated every corner of the devastated church. The candlelit ruins were majestic; eyes looked on with pride. Poland was reborn with Chopin's music.

When Sztompka, dressed in black, attacked the Polonaise in A-flat major, Op. 53, Madeleine reached out and held hands with Sainto beside her. Sainto, in turn, took Petit Bob's hand. Petit Bob took Tschupp's. A chain of sisterhood formed and tears flowed.

None of the twelve women would ever forget the Polonaise in A-flat major. That night, they were of one heart.

Chapter 13

NORMANDY-NIEMEN

(September–October 1945)

ucroquet received a new order, dated September 20, to travel to Silesia, not far from the Czech border, the formerly German region now being transferred to Poland. Commandant Ducroquet was vested with full powers to deal with all matters concerning the repatriation of French nationals. He had been asked by the French Embassy to set up a consular delegation in Wroclaw, a medieval-era city that, from 1741 to 1945, was a German city known as Breslau.

Breslau had been an impregnable fortress for the Germans, who had maintained a garrison of fifty thousand soldiers there. Between 1941 and 1945, the Gauleiter of Lower Silesia, Karl Hanke, enforced his rule with an iron fist, carrying out more than a thousand hangings to terrorize the population. The siege of Breslau by the Red Army began on February 15, 1945, and ended nearly three months later, on May 6, 1945, with the surrender of the German garrison, six days after that of Berlin.

The city was in ruins. Thousands of its inhabitants took part in the mass migration of Germans leaving the former German territories that were becoming part of Poland, but many Germans—Ducroquet stated 280,000 of them in the report he later wrote—stayed put, taking their chances on the new regime.

As soon as he arrived in the city, Ducroquet, wasting no time, made contact with the local authorities, as well as with the director of the cemeteries and the army colonel in command. The Polish administration in Lublin attached two Russian colonels to his team, supposedly to make his job easier, but, of course, to keep watch over him. Right away, he went to the main prison, on Opera Square, and saw that it was full of Germans, guarded by Poles, and foreign prisoners, guarded by Russians. He asked to see the prison files, hoping to find documentation on any French nationals among the foreign prisoners, but that was of no use, since the files were, at best, rough drafts; at worst, paper for lighting fires. The head guard, a German, was similarly useless. "He was able from time to time to provide interesting information because he had stayed in his post at this establishment during the entirety of the war," Ducroquet wrote in his report. "But after the Germans left, he had received such beatings from the Poles that he became disoriented, and he wandered around most of the time, with just brief flashes of lucidity, and I was thus able to extract virtually nothing from him." Ducroquet found himself, in other words, in a German town that had just been conquered by Soviet troops and entrusted to the Polish army—the entities often acting at loggerheads with each other.

Ducroquet left the prison and headed for the hospital. There, he knew, he was likely to find Alsatians, French nationals who had been drafted into the German army, but it was a tricky mission. How was he going to get the two Soviet colonels accompanying him to accept that men wearing Wehrmacht uniforms, and sometimes even Waffen SS uniforms, were Frenchmen who should be brought back to Paris?

There were, indeed, French nationals at the Wroclaw hospital. Ducroquet listed them: Joseph S., René W., Jacques B., Peter M., and Emil B. Two of the Alsatians, Alfonse S. and Jacques R., had already slipped away. Sanitary conditions were deplorable: typhus reigned, and the sick were scattered all over the place, even in the cellars of the town hall.

There were French graves everywhere: in public squares, in building courtyards, in gardens. Poor crosses adorned with tricolored paper marked the sites. On the crosses hung identity plates, each with the surname, first name, age, regiment, and service number of the deceased. With the help of Captain Birckel, who had come from Warsaw, Ducroquet made plans for the creation of a French cemetery.

Meanwhile, the task of repatriation was an arduous one. Some French survivors didn't wish to be identified. Many of them were afraid of returning to France—"with good reason," Ducroquet said, since at least some of these men had fought on the side of Germany during the war. They preferred to settle in Wroclaw. One day, as Ducroquet and

Birckel were canvasing from building to building, they came across a peeling house at 71 Klosterstrasse (the streets still bore their German names). They found two Frenchmen, Louis B. and Jean C., who had settled there with Polish wives.

When Ducroquet entered the house, he couldn't believe his eyes. There were paintings, bronzes, antique furniture, furs, and silverware. It was the Ali Baba cave of a fence, a person who collected and disposed of stolen goods. Ducroquet realized that Louis B. was the leader of a gang of looters, who combed the city and its environs, like the militiamen did in Paris during the Occupation. "The French have embedded themselves in the city where they live by looting, women, and theft," Ducroquet reported. The situation had changed, but the method remained the same. Exploiting the German debacle, Louis B. had collected files, documentation, and index cards. He had extended his tentacles all over the city.

But Ducroquet found that Louis B. was involved in something far bigger and more menacing than a mere fencing operation. In the report he wrote later, he told the curious story of what came to be called the "Dutch-Belgian committee" and his use of information obtained from Louis B. to fight against it. "He knew a lot," Ducroquet said of Louis B., specifically "a huge amount of documentation. That's why, despite the disgust that he inspired in me, I visited this individual, a civilian businessman, from time to time, making use of him for the particular purpose of ridding the city of the notorious 'Dutch-Belgian Committee.'"

Ducroquet learned that the Dutch-Belgian Committee, installed in a large building at 9 Bahnhofstrasse, was headed by a Belgian former SS man, who had stayed in Poland for the sake of a German girl. In return for large sums of money, these "scoundrels," as Ducroquet called them, issued authorizations for people, including former Nazis, to enter France or Belgium or Holland.

How? The committee was a criminal underground organization engaged in influence-peddling and false document procurement, carried out by former members of the Belgian SS and what Ducroquet called "the worst gang of hoodlums that I've ever encountered," including a member of the Russian command who provided protection for the racket. There was a workshop producing false identity cards, work certificates, census forms, demobilization records, and driver's licenses, all accompanied by the requisite authorization stamps from different government departments. It was the two Frenchmen, Louis B. and Jean C., living in their Ali Baba cave, who provided this information to Ducroquet, including the fact that the committee consisted of about fifteen members working under the Belgian SS officer's command. Those who called on the services of this group were generally Germans, mostly former SS, fleeing the Russian zone. They would pay "varying sums of money" for papers that would get them to France, Belgium, or Holland, and, presumably, from there to other countries. The Polish administration in Wroclaw was well aware of this criminal traffic, but they could do little to stop it, protected as it was by someone in the Russian command.

That, needless to say, made the situation very sensitive, but it was resolved, thanks to the support of the Belgians, who were anxious to avoid an influx of undesirables onto their soil. To get their coopera-tion, Ducroquet went across the Czech border to Prague, where France maintained a large official representation, including General Julien Flipo, the chief of staff of the French military mission in Czechoslovakia. Flipo introduced Ducroquet to the Belgian ambassador in Prague and then to a certain Colonel Henri (first name not disclosed in Ducroquet's report), who was in charge of Belgian security. As a result of these meet-ings, Ducroquet said, Brussels decided to "consider all members of the Dutch-Belgian committee as suspects." The meaning of this was clear: it was authorization for Ducroquet and the Belgian authorities to launch a large-scale operation in Wroclaw. Having gotten "the purely moral sup-port of the Polish authorities, while doing everything not to awaken the attention of the Soviets," Ducroquet and the Belgians, who possessed the necessary vehicles and armed personnel, went into action on the night of September 9. "The next morning before the sun was up," Ducroquet wrote, "the premises of the Belgian-Dutch Committee were surrounded and literally taken by assault. All the personnel were put into Belgian cars, with the exception of the mistress of the chief of the gang who suc-ceeded in escaping and ran to notify the Russian command. But when the [Russian] patrol arrived, the [Belgian] cars were already far away."

In the 1980s, I visited Poland, Hungary, Czechoslovakia, Romania, Bulgaria, and the USSR. My job was to negotiate film-distribution rights with all the countries of Eastern Europe. This was long after the war. The world had moved on, even if the Eastern bloc still held together. And yet, these trips—and the one to Poland in particular, of course—gave the stories my mother told me a new depth, as if the fact of being able to imagine events in settings I knew gave them an undreamed-of reality. It was only in the course of my investigation that I found episodes like this one, worthy of a novel—or a film. But I haven't gotten to Madeleine's deepest secret yet.

In Warsaw, it was a perpetual race against time. Every day brought its share of human heartbreak. Ambulances circulated, trains stopped and started, planes shuttled back and forth to Paris. Some mail from France arrived with gifts for Miche, celebrating her twenty-third birthday, a cigarette lighter and a camera. For the occasion, Roger Garreau performed a miracle. He found—God knows how—a chocolate cake! Perhaps it was the visitor who had arrived from France, a journalist from the newspaper *L'Aurore*, the Dawn, who had brought this delicacy? He was twenty-three years old, of Corsican origin—his name was Padovani, shortened to Pado on his byline—and he wielded a lively pen and exuded enthusiasm. He admired the work of the Blue Squadron. What was more, he had fallen in love with Petit Bob. With his clear eyes, he brooded over her and laughed every time she tried a bit of humor.

Pado's flirtation with Petit Bob was a welcome distraction from their ever-more-fraught situation. At the time, the fall of 1945, communications between French representatives in Poland and Moscow were very regular, which made the French well aware that the Soviets were not treating the border between themselves and Poland as a genuine international frontier, but were moving prisoners to the east, almost as if no border existed. Neither General Catroux's repatriation task, nor his dealings with the Soviet authorities, was easy. However, fate sometimes gave him a helping hand. One day, he became aware of a telegram addressed to Stalin, which, for the most part, was a standard message of congratulations for the great deeds of the "Little Father of Peoples." The letter was hardly a secret, nor did the Russian censors see anything wrong with it. However, Catroux noticed that it came from the leader of a Soviet prison camp, and hidden amidst the usual laudatory boilerplate—"father of peoples," "flower of spring," "beacon of doves," "great builder of communism," "you have the vigilance of the eye, the strength of the arm of those who watch over the interests of the father-land"—there was a nugget of information.

The telegram revealed that an operation was taking place in Murmansk, in the Barents Sea. Located two thousand kilometers north of Moscow, Murmansk had a special feature. Despite its position beyond the Arctic Circle, it was never icebound. The North Atlantic Drift, warmed by the Gulf Stream, provided the city with a relatively temperate climate. Upon inquiry, it was confirmed that a contingent of three thousand French nationals had somehow washed up in a camp near Murmansk, to be shipped off to an unknown destination. Catroux immediately dispatched one of his aides to investigate. When this person arrived in Murmansk, he realized that the prisoners had been moved from camp to camp for months, without any logical reason. The convoys set off, stopping at unknown stations, then headed back to forgotten towns, took forks leading southward, then were suddenly channeled northward, ending up on deserted steppes. Miraculously, Catroux recovered the men at Murmansk, after some hard bargaining, and got them onto an Allied ship.

Mission accomplished, but then another crisis appeared: a branch of the Red Cross in Odessa warned that a large contingent of French nationals there was in a terrible situation. These Frenchmen had married Russian women, and a hundred or so children had been born of these unions. The Soviet authorities were willing to allow the wives and children to follow their fathers to Odessa. But the families of these men could go no farther. Soviet law stipulated that a Russian citizen could only leave the country with the consent of the Supreme Soviet. Who, of course, never granted it. Unless they wanted to leave their families behind, these Frenchmen would never rejoin their homeland.

Madeleine and the Blue Squadron also had the opportunity—the temerity—to cross the Russian border, though not without difficulty and not without administrative difficulties. Heiniger, Miche, Braye, Pagès, Guillot, and Abbé Beilliard were all engaged in this mission, which involved a trip to the camp in Tambov, south of Moscow. Everyone was aware of the perilous situation, and a heavy silence reigned as the convoy approached the camp. They were stopped at a checkpoint.

"Where are you going?"

"We're looking for French nationals."

"There are none."

It was a familiar refrain. Things went wrong. The convoy was surrounded by soldiers. Everyone had to get out of the ambulances. Direction: the barracks for interrogation. The Russians treated the visitors like spies, and everyone at that point thought the mission was at a dead end. Worse, the French team wondered if they would suffer the same fate as the prisoners they'd come to rescue and disappear someplace in the East where they would never be found. But things were about to change.

The camp commander and the political commissar arrived, barking orders, resuming interrogations. It seemed the Russians were confiscating the entire convoy. But then, suddenly, Madeleine noticed a badge on the camp commander's uniform—two golden leopards on a field of crimson. She asked, "You wouldn't want to get the cousin of one of your Normandy-Niemen squadron heroes in trouble, would you?"

It was a magical reference. The Normandie-Niemen Fighter Squadron, formed in 1942 under the auspices of General de Gaulle, was a legend, one of only three Allied units that fought on the Russian front, credited with shooting down more than two hundred German aircraft. Men like Roland de La Poype and Albert Littolff fought valiantly in their aircraft, emblazoned with the two leopards that Madeleine saw on the Russian commander's uniform. Many of the French airmen paid the ultimate price in defense of the Russian homeland, and they were all awarded the Order of Lenin, the Order of the Red Flag, the Order of the Patriotic War, the Order of the Red Star, the Order of Alexander Nevsky.

Immediately, the hostile atmosphere was transformed. The Soviet commander looked at Madeleine, this young woman standing so proud, so determined, in front of him. When he saw the insignia of Free France on her jacket, he rushed to give her a hug, muttering, "Normandie-Niemen." For a time, he had been part of the quartermaster corps of the squadron, which had moved many times as the German army advanced and retreated. The moment was charged with emotion. The Russian soldiers stood still. Silence fell. Madeleine, her throat tight, felt the Russian kiss her on both cheeks. Then they looked into each other's eyes.

"There is such a thing as the brotherhood of arms," said Madeleine, touched.

The commander gestured broadly: "*Pa idiom*," he said. Let's get going.

As the Russian soldiers looked away, the girls, guided by Madeleine, rushed to the barracks. Five Frenchmen were there, quickly taken away. No one interfered. The Russian sentry at the entrance looked out over the horizon. There was a man on a stretcher, unconscious. Miche and Pagès lifted him. The ambulance doors slammed shut. The whole operation lasted just a few minutes.

Madeleine climbed back in. As the vehicle set off, she saw the Russian commander saluting, standing solemnly at attention. From her seat, she saluted, too. There are small miracles in life. Small miracles and coolness under fire.

In Warsaw, as in the rest of Poland, getting supplies was very complicated. Admittedly, since the regular arrival of planes, conditions had improved, but they were still sketchy.

What was most lacking was protein. Fresh meat was essential, but after the Soviet invasion, there had been no poultry anywhere, and the supply of pigs and oxen had been very undependable. Food from France or American stocks consisted mainly of dehydrated or canned vegetables. It was not much.

Madeleine recalled a tragi-comical incident that occurred shortly after her arrival. One evening, as squadron leader Ducroquet and Liber were sharing a frugal dinner, the door was kicked open. A Mongolian soldier entered. He looked around at the diners, then asked, "*Vratch?*" He wanted a doctor.

Ducroquet turned to the Mongol, who was a lieutenant in a tank unit.

"*Da.*" Yes.

Without another word, the visitor unbuttoned his trousers and placed his sexual organ, which was afflicted, onto a corner of the table.

The Mongolian lieutenant suffered from gonorrhea. And yet, in the Red Army, this disease—and all others that were sexually transmitted—could not be treated. That was the rule. This was because the communist authorities had long ago decreed that venereal diseases had officially disappeared from the USSR. What's more, since sexual relations with "women of foreign nationality" were outlawed (officially), the result was that "Russian venereals" went untreated, and if they did make their condition known, were punished. As a result, foreign doctors were under siege.

Ducroquet immediately saw the advantage of the situation. He knew that, in the satchel Liber had placed at the entrance, there were sulfonamides, but just as Liber reached for a handful of tablets—enough to treat an entire squadron—Ducroquet grabbed him by the arm.

"Just give him a little bit."

"Why?"

"Just two tablets."

Mixing English, French, and a few words of Russian, Ducroquet explained to the visitor that he would agree to give him two pills, but that if he wanted any more, he had to come back the next day, with meat.

"*Davaï!*" Agreed.

The next morning, there was a commotion—animal cries, human screams, and gunshots. Ducroquet looked out the window: several Ivans, accompanied by an old German and his son, were leading a cow and two pigs. Behind the soldiers, urging them on with his boots, the Mongol lieutenant was beaming, his face a picture of hilarity. He spotted Ducroquet and Liber in front of the mission and pointed to the animals:

"*Miaso!*" Meat!

Liber gave him two more tablets. The next day, the same.

And the day after that.

For a week, it was the same comedy. The whole hospital was jubilant.

Chapter 14

FORBIDDEN ZONES

(September–October 1945)

What a contrast between France celebrating its liberation and Poland still suffering! And all those French prisoners still moving in the wrong direction, on the verge of disappearing into the icy steppes of the USSR.

The young journalist Dominique Pado (who later became *L'Aurore*'s editor in chief and, after that, a member of the French Senate) wrote a series of articles in *L'Aurore* titled "Forbidden Zones" that was published at the end of September 1945. His descriptions of what he observed conveyed the harsh realities of Poland, bruised, battered, and overrun by Russian troops toughened by the hardships they'd endured.

When getting ready to cross the Polish border, he'd been greeted by machine-gun fire. When he finally managed to enter the country, all he saw was "the hallucinating, pitiful ghost of a nation that was once great." The Russian troops were numerous and intimidating, their "countless cattle cars decorated with scarlet stars, propaganda posters and . . . tobacco leaves drying in the sun or in coal dust." Pado continued: "It's all very dirty, and one wonders how human beings can live in such conditions. It's true that the Russian soldier has lived too long in the mud from Stalingrad to Berlin to worry about such things." What's striking is the fear he sensed—racial tensions, too. The three hundred thousand Jews still in Poland (compared to the three million there before the war) were being hunted down, not by Germans, but by Poles. When Pado entered a hotel, accompanied by a chaplain, the owner asked them what religion they were. The good abbot, completely disgusted, replied that he was a Buddhist. As for the journalist, he claimed to believe in Allah.

Finally, when he got to Warsaw, the devastation he saw, the rubble, the burned-out hulk of an entire city, was terrible.

"A crime against history," he wrote.

Pado continued to crisscross the country, painting a picture of what he saw, including his visit to the French mission in Warsaw, with Dr. Pauliac and the Blue Squadron, which left a lasting impression. He was astounded by the efforts being made to save "Frenchmen isolated in countless Soviet hospitals" and by the courage of the women who threw themselves into dangerous missions without the slightest hesitation. "They could boast of their exploits, but they never do," Pado wrote in his reverential account. "They could complain, but they don't even think of doing so." "When the weather gets really bad," he wrote, "the caravan stops and camps on the side of the road, the girls themselves in their cars lying on their stretchers. Only one of them stands guard against the possibility of an intrusion by the 'anti-Soviet partisans' that these regions are full of. And the redoubtable sentry paced back and forth, armed . . . with a little whistle."

Pado's admiration for the women of the squadron was intensified by his disdain for the hedonistic life that had taken over Paris in the wake of France's liberation. While most people, young and old, were engaged in "false joys, false inebriation," spending their time "laughing, dancing, and drinking," the eleven young women in Poland were, for him, a kind of model of self-sacrificing heroism. "Here it is, fourteen months without a break that they are saving human lives," he wrote in a page-one article in *L'Aurore*. The article showed a picture of two of the "Bleues" almost parallel to the ground as they leaned against the back of an ambulance, pushing it out of the mud.

They took roads "full of holes, encumbered with rubble to East Prussia, or to Silesia, or perhaps to the foothills of the Carpathian Mountains," and on their way back to Warsaw, "the beautiful cargo of amputated, wounded, and dying men behind them" joined them as "they sing the old songs that remind them of their country and of the past." It's a romanticized portrait that Pado painted, and it can't be forgotten that he fell in love with Petit Bob, even writing a letter to her father, on *L'Aurore* stationery, telling him that the Russians were posing

Figure 14.1   Page 1 of the newspaper *L'Aurore* with one of the journalist Dominique Pado's articles about the Blue Squadron, this one entitled "Eleven French Girls Sang." The subtitle reports, "They've saved thousands of men."

Figure 14.2 Micheline Reveron ("Miche") and Simone Saint-Olive ("Sainto") having a smoke at the entrance to the newly painted little house not far from the French Hospital in Warsaw, where the Blue Squadron was housed for most of their time in Poland.

an ever-graver danger to the Blue Squadron, which "can't help but get mixed up in the chaos." The "Ministry" in Paris, Pado said, speaking most likely of the Ministry of Prisoners, Deportees and Refugees, created in September 1944 to implement the repatriation agreement, had ordered the women to return to France for their safety, but the embassy in Warsaw had been postponing their departure week after week. "The gentlemen there want their company," Pado said.

The admiring portrait the journalist drew of the "Bleues" seems justified as the young women continued to comb the countryside. Sainto and Madeleine made their way to Prussia in rain that smelled of autumn, through looted towns without a soul to be seen. Sitting in the back, Pado took notes: "Barbed wire, ditches, hedgehogs. As far as the eye can see, it's a landscape of war. In the evening, Russian officers invite the girls to dinner, showing them a certain deference. The next day, the sun shines, but no French nationals are found."

At the end of September, the team headed for Krakow, with Abbé Beilliard. Arriving near the Black Madonna of Czestochowa, Madeleine stopped the ambulance. While the girls went to light a candle, she observed the surroundings. In the darkness of the basilica, the miraculous chapel was cluttered with donations, wishes, flowers, plates, and candles. Everywhere, stalls were selling pawned merchandise. For the women of the Blue Squadron, God had provided succor. Madeleine laughed gently every time she heard them appeal to Him in difficult times.

"And me?" she says. "Who do I dedicate myself to? To the moon."

Madeleine arrived at the French Hospital with two tuberculosis patients. They were in bad shape. It was the daily harvest. The next day, she picked up about fifteen Frenchmen, at the cost of the shock absorbers on her ambulance. The springboards were not made for these rough roads. Sometimes they broke and had to be repaired on the spot, "in the middle of nowhere," she added. Petit Bob's and Tschupp's hands were covered in grease as they deployed wrenches to dismantle the faulty parts, sometimes getting help from Russian troops, who rewelded the blades over tiny fires. The girls stuck together, their friendship stronger than ever. All those hours spent on the road, all those confidences exchanged, all those dangers incurred made for bonds that would never fade. Madeleine had won everyone's esteem; she was the soul of the squadron. She shone. The strength she possessed spread to them all. As Sainto wrote in her diary, "We'd die for her."

On October 4 came an alert: French nationals in Olsztyn had arrived not far from Warsaw. They were in danger of being taken away, so time was of the essence. Guillot woke everyone up at one o'clock in the morning. Sainto, sleepy-eyed, mumbled, "Petit Bob, take the wheel and hurry." Sainto dozed on her seat in the ambulance.

The other vehicles followed. Headlights swept through forests of birch, shedding their leaves. The weather turned foggy. What was summer dust turned to autumn mud. The kilometers rolled by, and Sainto, still asleep, was awakened at dawn by an exhausted Petit Bob, who whispered, "Take the wheel," and then collapsed. When they arrived, Guillot told Sainto that her ambulance had grazed a tree during the night. Petit Bob had almost fallen asleep while driving, but luckily, there was no accident. Providence?

With vehicles so severely tested by road conditions, incidents were commonplace. Once, Sainto was on her way to rescue Bray and Lagrange from some predicament, when suddenly her front wheel went missing. It just came off. After a quick stop, she was off to look for it, accompanied by the driver. In a rare instance, she was not with Petit Bob but rather the driver whom Sainto had put in his place after an inappropriate proposition to hitchhike back to Warsaw. When Sainto refused to leave the ambulance behind, he threw her his revolver and disappeared, wishing her good luck. It was going to be a long night. The Russians were bivouacked not far away, and Sainto had no wish to make herself known to them. She saw their campfires, their rifles, and as the night wore on, heard their songs getting louder and their voices thicker; the vodka was flowing. Sainto had seen so many women ruined, dirtied, and destroyed by Russian soldiers. All night long, she trembled with fear at being found out, keeping watch, waving her gun to dissuade cars from slowing down, until, finally, after her all-night vigil, she recognized a Blue Squadron ambulance, going the wrong way! The women told her they'd bumped into her driver in town, and though he hadn't raised any alarms, they'd pulled the truth out of him, then jumped into an ambulance and come to her rescue. Sainto got away with just a scare. "Tschupp, Blaise and my Petit Bob will always be my saviors," she wrote in her diary. "I'll always be grateful to them."

Figure 14.3 "The ambulances' springs weren't made for these rough roads. Sometimes they broke and we had to repair them on the spot." From left to right: Cécile Stiffler, Micheline Reveron, and Simone Saint-Olive, aka "Sainto."

Another day, Tschupp, this time accompanied by Madeleine, led the convoy in her vehicle. They were driving toward Warsaw at the end of the day. The bad weather had given way to beautiful autumn sunshine. The road bent westward. The light was blinding. The shadows were long. Suddenly, the ambulance in front of Sainto's vanished. Sainto slammed on the brakes.

Tschupp and Madeleine's vehicle had fallen into empty space. A bridge had been blown up.

Everyone rushed to help. Tschupp was able to hang on to the door handle as the vehicle plunged into the abyss. Madeleine, on the other hand, banged her head against the windshield, and her hands were now full of shards of glass. Her rib cage was also damaged, and she couldn't move. Blood was running down her face.

The friends rushed in. Petit Bob opened the door, and the doctor's body slowly tilted toward her. Guillot stretched out her arms; Madeleine's head lolled back. Her eyes were open but empty. They laid her on the floor, and Guillot examined her. Her pulse was weak. Her belt had to be loosened, the pressure points released. Tschupp removed Madeleine's shoes.

She was breathing.

Was her rib cage crushed? On touching it, Guillot realized that one or two ribs were probably broken. Painful, but not fatal. It was the head that was particularly worrying. Tschupp was petrified, her hand over her mouth, knowing that as the driver, the responsibility for what happened would be hers. Madeleine, now lying on a stretcher, complained of a headache.

Figure 14.4   Vilette Guillot became an expert in vehicle repair, which was a good thing given how frequently the ambulances broke down.

"What happened?" she asked.

They explained it to her, their relief palpable, their emotions intense. There was an instant of silence, and then cheers erupted.

"Madeleine! You scared us! We thought . . . !" and, behind the demonstration of joy, Sainto's voice was soft:

"You know, Madeleine, we love you."

Later, she asked Sainto to take an X-ray of her skull. She diagnosed a fracture there herself. The line was clearly visible. She casually told the worried team, "I used to ski a lot. Once, I fell into a tree." This was the second time she'd cracked her skull.

But she suffered, silently. Behind the good-natured joking, there was pain. Pagès gave her a shot of morphine. A few days later, with her

Figure 14.5 Jeanine Robert, aka "Petite Bob," gets her hands greasy.

hair cut short and her head bandaged, she tried to stand and abruptly collapsed. She was scolded, advised to lie down, to wait, to rest, even to return to France. But Dr. Pauliac was adamant. There was no way she was going to lose any of the precious time remaining.

Deep down, Madeleine knew the mission was largely up to her. She knew its twists and turns, its dark areas, its secrets. If she left the ship, it risked going adrift, and there was still work to be done. Everyone was counting on her, especially the latest arrivals—like Mlle. Collet.

Mlle. Collet (her first name is unknown) arrived from France in August as a reinforcement, but she immediately took charge of putting the hospital in order, and she did it well. She was spirited, full of energy, and courageous, but "life has treated her terribly," noted Sainto, who had evidently been the repository of some undisclosed confidences. The woman who had become the hospital's "supreme manager" was very attached to the "Bleues," and particularly to Madeleine.

The pace of operations quickened again. Everyone sensed that with the onset of winter, access to the camps and hospitals where French nationals remained would become more difficult. Madeleine ordered a mission to Pulavy in the south, and despite the protests of the others that she was not yet ready to go back into action, she imposed her will. Madeleine suffered in silence, though Pagès gave her a shot of morphine. She made her decision to keep going despite the pain. She refused to be repatriated after the accident, minimizing its seriousness, describing what was a fracture of her skull as a simple contusion. It was October; she didn't go back to France until December, and her suffering during that stretch of time was enormous.

When the ambulance arrived at its destination in Pulavy, a town on the road to Lublin, the squadron found that the camp there was entirely manned by Russians, all of them drunk. The mission took a farcical turn when the local commander, a pharmacist from Stalingrad in civilian life, asked Madeleine to marry him. Because of her head injury, she was wearing a kind of Arab princess turban, which seemed to arouse romantic feelings in him. The situation was unforeseen in other ways, as well: the fellow was as naked as a worm. As the libations continued, the situation resolved itself. The Russians drank toasts to the Frenchwomen, but the women had a strategy to avoid falling into the alcohol trap. They clinked their glasses in a kind of relay, while the Russians downed their vodka with each toast. Soon the Russians passed out, the Blues located the French prisoners they had come to retrieve and the ambulances left with them inside.

The cold set in, and the Vistula began to freeze.

In the evenings, conversations between the doctors and some of the patients took a literary turn, with Captain Jean Neurohr. In a haze of cigarette smoke, they evoked the works of Gide, Mauriac, and Sartre, as well as those of Pierre Benoit and a young author, Guy des Cars. Nights passed, filled with hopes, confidences, bitterness, memories and friendship, while the clogged hospital toilet overflowed into the kitchen. Sainto took part in the conversation. She'd read *Le Silence de la Mer*, the novel written during the Occupation by Vercors (a pen name for Jean Bruller) about a German officer billeted in a village with a retired Frenchman and his niece, both of whom vow never to speak to him. Sainto was seduced by Vercors's prose—"A leader who doesn't love his people is a miserable mannequin." And then, "A leader who loves his people doesn't need authority; following him is a matter of course." When the German officer departed for the front, the Frenchman left him a quotation from the writer Anatole France—"It is a fine thing when a soldier disobeys a criminal order."

"By the way," said Madeleine, "did you know that Aragon was here the other day?" She was talking of Louis Aragon, the famous surrealist poet (and member of the French Communist Party). "He spent a night at the embassy. He was on his way to Moscow, but his pilot refused to go any further. We found him at the airfield, not happy at all." Neurohr found a copy of *Les Yeux d'Elsa* by Aragon—Elsa's Eyes, and he read from it. "The sky is never as blue as it is over the wheat." The phrase still rings in Sainto's ears when she writes in her notebook, "Everything in Poland is immense. The landscape, the silence, the whiteness, the birch woods, the climate, typically continental with a hot summer and a cold, rainy autumn. Winter will be icy in the Carpathians."

From Paris, she had just received Pado's front-page article in *L'Aurore*, titled "*Onze filles de France chantaient*"—Eleven girls from France sang. "I'm thinking in particular of the eleven young French girls I met, more than thirty days ago, far from home, over there, in the land of Poland," Pado wrote. "Tonight, as this autumn day fades, I see them

Figure 14.6   Aline Tschupp and Madeleine on the balcony of the French Hospital in Warsaw, after the ambulance Madeleine was riding in plunged into an abyss. Madeleine diagnosed herself with a fractured skull, but she kept on working.

again, in their little house in Warsaw, just fifty meters from the muddy, reddish Vistula. . . . They always have a young, cheerful heart. And when, in the ruins, the Polish men and women meet them, dressed in their blue uniforms, they turn around to hear the clear laughter of these young girls from France."

These interludes enabled Madeleine and the eleven young women to regain their footing in "normal" life, because danger always awaited around the next bend in the road. And sometimes it was their foolhardiness that put them in danger—or their mad courage.

Since Fouchet's departure from Warsaw, Madeleine had remained in contact with his confidential correspondent, and this person had now passed along a crucial piece of information from a secret contact he had in the Lublin government. The Soviets would be closing the borders in mid-November. The French mission in Warsaw would have to pack up.

The message from the contact in Lublin, written in French, added that this would be his last sign of life. From now on, he would no longer exist. Poland, which had entered the iron age of communism, was closing down. The era of near-détente between it and the Allies was over, and the small window that had opened with the agreements on the repatriation of prisoners in June 1945 had been slammed shut.

It was a shocking revelation, coming with such suddenness. The French Hospital had never been so full of wounded as it was now, but the Ministry of Prisoners, Deportees and Refugees, created on September 1, 1944, to implement the repatriation agreement, was going to be abolished on November 14, 1945.

And so it was that on November 11, 1945, the Blue Squadron was officially disbanded.

The girls were once again on the road heading back to France. No doubt, there was some kind of going-away ceremony at the hospital or embassy, but none of the "Bleues" seems to have mentioned it. Sainto, however, evoked her distress that the mission was being dissolved while "there are still so many abandoned men," though she admitted that winter had come, making their rescue extremely difficult anyway. On November 11, they were on their way back to France, driving their five rugged ambulances on roads now underneath a covering of new snow, retracing more or less the route they had taken eight months earlier to Warsaw—through the Carpathian Mountains, across the Czech border to Prague, on to the French city of Dijon, where Micheline Reveron's parents lived. They must have said goodbye there, each taking a different route to their various destinations.

But Madeleine remained behind in Warsaw for a little longer, on the pretext that she had some administrative work to take care of, though it is probably safe to assume that she was simply reluctant to leave with so many people still under her care, so much left to do. And then, when she was finally ready to make her departure, she discovered there would be an unexpected and unavoidable delay. The now almost-palpable descent of the Iron Curtain had prompted panicky foreigners to make plans to leave Poland while they still could—and with heavy snow covering the roads, the only exit was by one of the few flights taking off from Warsaw. "Sainto, my big girl, I finally left Warsaw with its icicles and snow in true Warsaw style—everybody was going up to the airfield,

revolver in their pockets intending to use it"—meaning not guns literally, but that everybody was ready to fight to get onto an airplane.
"Twenty-one journalists have been stamping their feet for three weeks,"
Madeleine continued. "The arrival of a second plane saved everything;
there would surely have been deaths otherwise." Even then the danger
was not over. "In Berlin, visibility was near zero. We found ourselves
suddenly in front of a factory chimney that our plane narrowly avoided.
The right wing ripped off an antenna further on."

With her departure, Madeleine left behind a French contingent
stripped to its essentials. Liber had left in July. Ducroquet had gone home
in one of the ambulances driven by the "Bleues." Still at their posts were
Ambassador Garreau, Commander Neurohr, and Collet, no doubt to
continue running the hospital. But except for that, the French mission
was over. In a letter, dated December 13, from Captain Neurohr, who
was still in Poland, he told Madeleine, "I regretted not having been able
to have a long talk with you before your departure, but the last days
of your stay in Warsaw were so hectic." In the same letter, the captain
reported that he hadn't heard from the "Bleues" yet. He missed them,
"especially Tschupp, Petit Bob, and Sainto." In Warsaw, he reported, it
got dark before 4 p.m., the electricity was cut off, candles were used for
lighting; you had to buy charcoal at the "free market." Reading these
simple words, Madeleine was plunged back into the atmosphere of "over
there." The sense of service, the camaraderie, the solidarity among the
members of her band.

She was lonely—terribly lonely. At Christmas, after a couple weeks
in Paris, she returned home.

Chapter 15

HER LAST CHRISTMAS

(December 1945)

Outside, snow covered the streets of Villeneuve-sur-Lot, and only a few Christmas lights in the windows marked the festive season. The freeze, which had been raging for the past fortnight, had turned the milk bottles into solid blocks, and the cobblestones were slippery under the horses' feet. It was a Christmas like before the war, with the family huddled around the fireplace, oranges under the tree, and, with a bit of luck, a goose roasting in the oven. For the rest, it was a case of getting by as best you could. In France at the end of 1945, everything was in short supply: butter, sugar, flour, coffee. The only commodity available without restriction was wine. From Algeria or Languedoc, it flowed freely.

Madeleine, standing in the doorway, inhaled the icy air and smiled. After all, this harsh winter was nothing compared to Polish winters. She put her hand to her forehead. At times, her fracture caused stabbing pain, but then it diminished gradually.

While her grandmother busied herself in the kitchen, Madeleine entered the house, sat down in a tired, old armchair, and silently contemplated the blazing fire. The dry wood, chestnut, crackled and sparked. Roger Pauliac's photo was on the mantelpiece. She looked at it, then closed her eyes. Poland was in her heart. Letters from some of the "Bleues" had arrived from Paris. All were in the same state of mind. They missed the action; a feeling of uselessness clung to them. Some of them were already thinking of leaving again, of getting involved elsewhere, even if their families were not enthusiastic.

My mother, Anne-Marie, sat down beside her sister, and the clock chimed in the silence. Voices were heard from the kitchen; everyone was buzzing with talk. The house was in a joyful sort of disorder. For this first Christmas of freedom, we'd pulled out all the stops. And never mind the food stamps still in force; the restrictions would have to wait. The atmosphere was one of gaiety and palpable relief. The night wore on amidst bursts of laughter, good wishes, gifts, and hugs. There was also a new baby, my older sister, Marie-Laure.

Most of all, the prodigal daughter's return was being celebrated. She was constantly being questioned, congratulated, encouraged, and asked for details. *What happened in Warsaw? Are the Russians as barbaric as they say? What's there to eat in Poland? Who are the French who stayed behind? Should the collabos and Malgré-nous be shot? What was the most memorable part of the mission?* In snatches, Madeleine did her best to explain.

Something similar was happening in the other households of the "Bleues" and others newly back from Warsaw. No doubt Liber was also at a festive table, in Walincourt, where he had returned. He did so somewhat reluctantly, but he yielded to his family's entreaties to fulfill his duty to succeed his father as a country doctor. Liber had finished five years of captivity only a few short months before, and he wanted to resume a normal life. It was typical for a doctor in a family medical practice to be married, which was what his parents were urging him to do. And he did marry, in February 1946. Ironically, Liber and his bride, who later became his medical secretary, were enjoying their honeymoon when Madeleine had her fatal car accident.

The other "Bleues" were also returning to normal life that Christmas. Petit Bob raised a glass at home with her parents and sister; Sainto in Lyon was getting ready to go to midnight mass. Madeleine thought of Tschupp, who provided so much comfort after her accident, and of the others—the courageous Blaise, Abbé Beilliard, and Roger Garreau, whom she was supposed to meet again soon.

The house in Villeneuve-sur-Lot was now silent. It was 2 a.m. The two sisters had decided to sleep together, as they'd once done, in their girls' room, on the second floor. At the end of the hallway, the Louis XVI twin-bedded room, with its hand-painted gray posts, remained as it had been. Grandmother had forbidden any changes to the décor. The cognac had had its effect; there was nothing left of the goose; and the fire in the fireplace had slowly died down. Standing by her bed, Madeleine looked at the ghostly design drawn by the frost on the windowpane, as if hinting at some kabbalistic mystery. The distant countryside gleamed faintly in the moonlight.

"I find you very thin; you don't look well," Anne-Marie told her sister.

Madeleine didn't reply. Instead, she said, "You don't know how much it means to me to be reunited with my family and nephews. Marie-Laure, what a beautiful baby!"

"I gave birth without you, Madeleine, two weeks ago. Why did you stay longer in Poland? The Blue Squadron girls returned a month ago; you could have been there for the birth . . . and Gilles," she added, speaking of Madeleine's fiancé. "It's time to build your life." (We don't have much information about Gilles, who was likely still in America.)

Anne-Marie had been keeping close watch on her sister, seeing that each time Madeleine answered the eager questions coming from her curious family members, a brief mist of melancholy passed over her eyes. It was as if she was holding something back. She was there at home with her family, but not totally there, and my mother saw it, something blocked in Madeleine, something repressed. For the past few days, she'd been offering comfort to her sister, who wouldn't open up. True, she told stories, but she was leaving something in the shadows. There was a kind of concealed emotion, sadness, revulsion, worry, horror, struggle. It was no longer about medicine, Anne-Marie thought; it was about healing souls. Not in the religious sense. In the simplest, most material sense, relieving suffering.

"You're not going back there?" Anne-Marie asked; she was a bit incredulous as, suddenly, she guessed the question that had been on Madeleine's burdened mind.

"Yes, I have to," Madeleine admitted, knowing Anne-Marie would greet this news with dismay and opposition.

"Oh no, you're not going back! The war is over, the Red Cross is over, Poland is over! Don't go!"

"It's not over, Anne-Marie, not over at all." Anne-Marie knew deep down that her sister's mission was, and still is, very important. She knew that the work accomplished was fundamental, and she sensed the extent to which Madeleine had invested herself in it. But how could she not be afraid to see her sister return to a country that she'd described as completely destroyed, still in the grip of a terrible violence? And with the Iron Curtain rapidly descending? Life also had to be restored back home after the long years of occupation.

Anne-Marie got up, approached Madeleine, took her by the shoulders, and the two of them, in their nightgowns, contemplated the lunar landscape, gently swept by flakes swirling around the bell tower in the distance. Time passed slowly. When Madeleine finally pulled back to sit on the edge of the bed, Anne-Marie could see that the tears were flowing.

"What's the matter, Madeleine? What's the matter?"

"It's over there."

"Over there? In Poland?"

"Yes."

"What is it? Tell me."

"Promise me you'll never talk about it."

"I swear."

"It's important, Anne-Marie. Really important."

Madeleine wiped her tears, and her story spilled out, a story of misfortune and fear that had to be kept secret. It had to do with the nuns from the convent in the forest near Warsaw and how Madeleine had answered their call when they came to see her after Abbé Beilliard's mass.

In the darkness, the two nuns, without a word, showed her the way. The forest rustled in the wind. Occasionally, an animal whose eyes glowed in the darkness crossed in front of the headlights. Listening only to her heart as a woman and her mind as a doctor, she came alone, as she had been asked.

The monastery was a low building with an inner courtyard around which the nuns' cells were arranged. A chapel in poor condition adjoined the presbytery, which contained a meeting room, refectory, workshop, laundry, kitchen, and infirmary. The roof slates were irregular, the walls oozed dampness, and weeds grew between the slabs of the Stations of the Cross. The only well-kept spot: the vegetable garden. The smell of incense and earth lurked everywhere.

What struck Madeleine as she entered the place was the silence, which seemed to her even more profound than in other convents she had visited. And she soon found out why.

The Mother Superior related the story that Madeleine now told, the emotion in her voice, to Anne-Marie, a story all the more terrible for not being unique in the Poland of that moment. Like the nuns Madeleine had met on her trip to Danzig, all the nuns in this monastery near Warsaw had been raped—all of them. First it was by a unit of routed German soldiers who, though fleeing in disarray ahead of the Soviet advance, imposed no limits on their wanton depredations; then it was by soldiers of the Red Army, determined to make the most of their victory by looting, burning, and raping. They came back ten times, twenty times, thirty times to take advantage of their "trophies." Some of the sisters were dead; others would have preferred it. Some had venereal diseases; others were torn apart. All the clinical pictures of unbearable violence were present before Madeleine's eyes.

Some of the nuns were pregnant; some had already given birth.

The Mother Superior was desperate for help with the newborns and with the sisters who were about to give birth. It was such a dramatic situation that she took the risk of telling someone. She chose Madeleine because she was a woman and a foreigner. There was less risk in that than in telling the authorities.

There had to be absolute secrecy. And Madeleine was committed to preserving it.

"Why was Mother Superior so adamant that nothing of what had happened in the convent be known outside of its walls?" Anne-Marie couldn't help interrupting her sister to ask that question, and she was shocked by what Madeleine told her in response.

When Russian troops were deployed, they first settled their scores with the Germans. Then politics took over, politics and ideology. Religious schools were closed, and several thousand nuns were forced to abandon their convents and become public schoolteachers. On the surface, the Russians pretended to reach a *modus vivendi* with the Polish Church and the Polish primate, Archbishop Hlond. In 1941, Archbishop Hlond had complained to Cardinal Maglione in Rome that Pope Pius XII had abandoned Polish Catholics. After the war, in light of the crimes committed by the Soviets, Hlond issued a pastoral letter: "Not since the days of St. Peter has the Church been the object of such intense persecution as it is today." The fire spread: in Hungary, eight hundred monks and seven hundred nuns were driven from their monasteries in the middle of the night. In Poland, almost a thousand nuns were told they could no longer work in hospitals. Some were deported to the USSR. Charitable organizations were closed. According to the communists, they had been infiltrated by "aristocrats" and Nazi sympathizers. Clearly, they were now in the crosshairs of the new regime. In the new world emerging behind the Iron Curtain, the Church was a cancer to be eradicated.

"So that's it," Madeleine concluded. "The Mother Superior didn't want to draw attention to her convent. The sisters survive by trying to make themselves forgotten."

From that first night onward, Madeleine returned as often as she could to look after the nuns—those who had become mothers, of course, as well as delivering the babies and caring for them. She tended to the other women's ailments as well. She didn't ask questions. "Do you understand, Anne-Marie? I could never have imagined such a situation." No one could have imagined.

The fire in the bedroom's small fireplace had gone out. Night covered everything. Madeleine's face, indistinct in the darkness, was soft when Anne-Marie caressed her cheek.

"Continue."

According to the monastic rule in force then, nuns were not allowed to strip naked; when they bathed, once a month, they did so wearing long linen shirts over their bodies. They were forbidden to touch "shameful parts." They had never seen a shower. Daily washing was perfunctory, with a square of cloth and a little cold water in a basin, and it only involved the face, never the middle of the body. Soap was rare, almost nonexistent.

Madeleine felt as if she had returned to the Middle Ages.

She taught the basics of maternity to the first of the women who gave birth—how to change their babies, wash them, breastfeed, hold and cuddle them. Whenever possible, Madeleine took the car and slipped away from the clinic and repatriation center in Warsaw. Once at the convent, she treated the most urgent cases. Then she had to help the mothers. Madeleine did the best she could with what she had, but the shattered intimacies, the psychological ravages, the pervasive sense of dislocation, she would deal with later. The community of sisters had been devastated by an inner fire, by a secret catastrophe.

There was no question of going to the authorities. On the one hand, this was because of the opprobrium that would have fallen on these raped women; on the other, it was because of their religious status, as this was viewed by the ideologists in Lublin. In the eyes of Marxist politicians, the nuns were nothing more than parasites on the working class, to be eliminated as quickly as possible. What was more, it would have been unthinkable to spread the word that the Red Army was a bunch of rapists. So, the situation, unspeakable as it was, had to be handled carefully, very carefully.

Madeleine told her sister about her fear of being caught every time she visited. She was physically exhausted, because she attended to the nuns at night and performed her duties at the French Hospital during the day. She was forced to tell lies when asked questions. She'd really have liked to have been able to confide in someone, share the horror that she'd seen at the convent, gain moral support for the work she was doing there. But she'd promised not to say anything to anybody and to help the nuns to "free their conscience," that is, to take responsibility for the terrible choice they were going to have to make concerning their babies, born of rape, but who were now also sacred and unique.

Back in Warsaw, some were beginning to wonder about Madeleine's absences. It was important for her not to arouse suspicions, especially given that relations with the Ivans were already strained. Madeleine stayed at the hospital for two nights, not going to the convent. Her face was haggard, dark circles formed around her eyes, but she did her examinations, and she saw everything and everyone—German women came to her asking to be sent to Switzerland by the Red Cross on the pretext that they were certainly suffering from tuberculosis; another woman, from Bavaria, was a piano teacher. The French, she said, should do something for the Germans, who, she claimed with seeming sincerity, had behaved well. She even had the names of French citizens she knew if the need should have arisen. At that, Madeleine felt her anger rising.

"And the crematoria?"

"But there were also poor Germans who fell victim."

Anne-Marie got up. Madeleine, wrapped in her quilt, sat on the bed. The clock on the wall said six in the morning. Christmas was over. The cold crept in through the gaps in the window. But the past was still with them.

"I must admit that the term 'poor Germans' didn't go over very well."

"I understand."

As their physical problems were dealt with, the nuns gave birth, and their babies' lives were assured, Madeleine wondered what came next. While some of the sisters had developed a maternal instinct despite the appalling circumstances, others rejected their children and wouldn't even feed them. And children in a monastery were not going to go unnoticed, despite the nuns' discretion.

"Understand, Anne-Marie. The situation was awful. The babies were the fruit of sin, the living proof of their degradation, obvious reminders of their forbidden relationship to the flesh, the negation of virginal purity, original sin in all its horror."

Day broke. A pale glow rubbed off the darkness of the night. Anne-Marie looked at her sister, speechless.

"Shall we go to the kitchen for coffee?"

"If you'd like."

The two sisters got up, put on their slippers, and went downstairs. The old house creaked under their feet, but nothing moved. Anne-Marie was standing at the stove, heating the water. Madeleine sat down in front of the washed-out table, where dishes from the day before were piled up, and placed two bowls in front of her. The smells of roasting, fruit, wax, and smoke mingled. That was what Christmas was all about, that special aroma of home and food.

With coffee poured and sugar stirred, Madeleine resumed her story.

"I came up with a plan. We had to allow the nuns who wanted to keep their babies to do so without drawing attention to themselves. So, I came up with the idea of creating an orphanage in the convent itself."

It was an ingenious idea, one of those ideas you think is obvious once someone has thought it up, but it wasn't obvious at all at the time. But it would save everything and solve all the problems at once. The nuns wouldn't be torn away from their children. They could stay with them, presumably taking care of orphans, so the opprobrium of it all wouldn't touch them.

Madeleine was in the ideal position to set up this orphanage: she was a doctor, with all the authority that status conferred. And to be a foreign doctor was a great help, since a foreign doctor could receive support from other foreigners, as well as from the Polish Red Cross, with which she had a very close relationship. And then there were so many little orphans wandering the streets of Warsaw whose misery could also be alleviated and who would help in disguising the conditions of the nuns, since to seem like a real orphanage, the one Madeleine created needed to have children of all ages, not just newborns.

"So, they were all able to stay?"

"Just about. But some mothers didn't want their children. We had to come up with something else, especially as living conditions there were tough, and means were very limited. So, I thought of a way. The American ambassador, Arthur Bliss Lane, helped me. He was revolted by the way the Allies had abandoned Poland. And the fate of the children was unbearable for him. The American Red Cross provided us with logistics. And so did Mr. Christians, president of the Polish Red Cross. We rounded up twenty-four children in the greatest secrecy; some were children of the nuns, others orphans from Warsaw. And we evacuated them in small groups to be flown back to France."

"What happened to them?"

"They were taken in hand, discreetly, and dispersed among French families. The hospital network I had been a part of in Paris took care of it. Everything was done clandestinely."

"Are you going to go back?"

"I promised I would."

When the household woke up, Madeleine was sitting at the old piano in the living room. As the family surrounded her, she began to play Chopin's Polonaise in A-flat Major.

Snow fell.

Chapter 16

BACK HOME
(December 1945–January 1946)

For all the women, the return to "normal" life involved a difficult adjustment, from their life of danger, excitement, and meaning to the ordinary, with its comforts and relative dullness. "As expected," wrote Petit Bob to Madeleine in a letter dated December 24, 1945, "yesterday we were at a surprise party, and the atmosphere was very nice. It's weighing me down, and yet I'm spoiled and pampered by everyone, but I feel as if I'm suffocating."

For her part, Madeleine wrote to Sainto, "I found my Petit Bob worried, not happy, unadapted to family life, crying while waiting for her Sainto."

The correspondence between the young women of the Blue Squadron and Madeleine began the day after the former's departure from Warsaw. On November 12, the day after leaving Warsaw, Tschupp wrote Madeleine a letter beginning, "Little doctor, darling." Tschupp maintained a sense of humor and detachment, even if it was a bit forced, and the melancholy seeped out. She said the girls went shopping in Wroclaw, which was diverting, but she didn't suppress her sense of nostalgia or the sadness she felt at leaving Madeleine in Warsaw. "I leave you, dear little doctor, with regret, like yesterday, hoping despite it all to see you again in the very near future. I embrace you with all my heart."

On January 15, 1946, at home in Lille, Squadron Leader Ducroquet took up his best pen, beginning a letter to Madeleine with "*Tovaritch*

Phénomène"—phenomenal comrade. Then after he sacrificed himself to custom and presented his wishes for the coming year, he evoked "our tête-à-tête dinners" and tried his hand at humorous disengagement ("I'm an idiot, I know. I always have been, and I've never regretted my idiocy. . . . I'm suffocating. I'm bumping into everything"). He asked for a photo, and before signing off as "an admirer," he wrote, "don't go. Stay with us. Why drive to Germany, Austria, or China? With whom? For what? For whom?" He pressed on: "I'm not a priest, but I'd like to hear your confession. What big indelible sin could there be on this little white soul?" He ended his three-page letter, "Don't go off to the devil like that, on your own. It's true that I'll never be able to go with you. I'm definitely out of sorts."

Madeleine told Sainto about this letter: "I've just received a large letter from your father (Commandant Ducroquet). He wrote on the envelope, '*Faire suivre même en Chine*'—Forward, even to China. Inside was his photo with this dedication: 'To MP the strangest phenomenon I have ever met.'"

On January 21, Ducroquet wrote to Madeleine again, this time saluting her in teasing fashion as "*Tovaritch Vibrion*"—meaning a person nervous or agitated. The handwriting was less neat, the calligraphy more jagged. "This is it! That's the hardest blow I could have taken! You're leaving, just like that, for Warsaw, as if you were going to the suburbs! Isn't there anyone around to grab you by the arm and send you to the corner? Is there any reason to let little girls run the roads of Europe?"

So Madeleine was returning to Warsaw, and the consternation that her decision provoked among her family and the members of her former team added to the mystery of her return. Why would she go back, this woman of thirty-three with a fiancé and every reason to devote herself now to private life? Everybody was against it—her grandmother, her mother, and her beloved sister, who entreated her to stay. Poland had closed itself off to the outside world. The Iron Curtain had fallen. All of Madeleine's contacts in Paris, Minister Fouchet and the "Warsavians," Ducroquet and the other "Bleues" who had returned to France—all advised her not to go. In addition, the winter of 1945 was very harsh and the car journey dangerous.

And yet, Madeleine defied their wise counsel and their entreaties. Perhaps the mere fact that Gilles was going to Switzerland played a role. Why not take care of matters in Poland as long as he was going to be gone for a while anyway? But Madeleine's remarkable devotion to duty and to afflicted Poland had to be the main explanation. Before leaving France, she went for a few days on a confidential trip to London, a city with which she had no known prior connection and where it is likely that she met with representatives of the Polish government in exile who had information and documents to pass on to the non-communist Poles still trying to resist the fait accompli of the communist takeover of the country. Madeleine also had information for Ambassador Garreau and Colonel Poix, the military attaché. In addition, she had seen to the transfer to France of the "orphan" children of raped nuns and no doubt she wanted to give them news of these children, to reassure them and the Mother Superior that they were being adopted by French families. And then, she had promised Collet, the "manager" of the French Hospital, she would return to complete reports and administrative tasks. The hospital had changed status; it was no longer reserved only for French nationals, but open to the general population of Warsaw.

In addition, the Polish Red Cross, which, in October, had awarded Madeleine the Golden Cross, had asked her to extend her stay. "It is with great pleasure that we would accept the appointment of Mlle Pauliac," the letter said, "so devoted to our compatriots, as delegate to the Polish Red Cross so that we can continue our mutual collaboration." Christians then "proposed to extend Mlle. Pauliac's stay in Poland," a strong sign that high among her reasons to return to Warsaw was the request of the Polish Red Cross that she do so.

Finally, there were still these thousands of French people, soldiers, forced laborers and *malgré-nous*, still prisoners in camps or held in hospitals, and there were thousands of French families still hoping for their return.

She shouldn't have done it. It was a tragic mistake to return to Poland. But Madeleine Pauliac, who had followed her own star all her life, followed it to Poland, with tragic consequences.

Meanwhile, France was slowly reawakening. General de Gaulle, who had led the provisional government of France since the Liberation in

1944, tendered his resignation to the president of the National Assembly on January 20, 1946. "I'm out of here," he said expressing his frustration with the petty factionalism of party politics. With his sudden departure, de Gaulle began his crossing of the political desert, waiting for his country to call him to the rescue once again (which it did in 1958), but in the meantime, signaling the country's step toward its postwar future. The big hit in the movies was *La Bataille du Rail* (The Railroad Battle), starring Charles Boyer, about the heroic efforts of French rail workers to sabotage German military transports during the war. Tino Rossi sang "*Petit Papa Noël*," as the country took on a kind of good-times-are-here-again mood, represented by Édith Piaf's smash hit "*La Vie en Rose*"—Life in Pink.

La vie en rose, really?

For Madeleine, at least, life just before heading back to Warsaw did sometimes seem pink. She wrote to Sainto on January 1 to tell her that just before she was due to leave on a ski vacation in the Tyrol, her fiancé, Gilles, had arrived from America. But in just two days, he was leaving again, this time for Singapore. "I'm flying with him to Lyon or Valence, depending on the weather," she said in her letter. "Gilles is worth all the Tyrols in the world. If I could, I would go further." A few weeks later, a week before leaving for Warsaw, she wrote, "Gilles is not on the path to my heart, he's in it."

But Poland left a void in the hearts of all of the women. Their lives resumed, but what lives? There were no broken roads, or Russian dangers, or spooky forests, or men to save, or embers of war, all of which they missed, inexplicably perhaps, along with the sense of urgency and apprehension that had accompanied them every day during their mission. For some, in the face of the everyday banal, a kind of melancholy took hold.

From Paris, Petit Bob wrote to Madeleine, "Dear Doctor and friend," she said, adopting the more formal *vous* form of address, rather than the informal *tu*. "For 1946, I've decided to live a little less with the past, without forgetting it, and I'd like to regain my old zest for life. Will I succeed?"

Around the same time, Sainto took up her pen in Lyon: "Hi toubib of my heart," she began, using the Arabic word for "doctor." "Despite my fickle and unfaithful airs, I think of you very often. My nose red, my fingers cold, my hair a mess, I'm thinking hard so that I can see you in my imagination without having to worry about you.

"Bob told me on the phone that you almost lost the rest of your hair. How awful! I'm so much happier knowing you're away from the Tovaritchs! Seeing your handwriting again brought back a whole past. What beautiful memories! Good memories, thanks to you! I seem to talk about you all the time, and in such terms that the whole family just wants to get to know you! See you soon, my dear tovaritch major. . . . I kiss you with all my heart."

A few days later, she wrote again:

> My dear little doctor, Are you still in this much pain? It's hopeless that there are so many kilometers between Paris and Lyon, because then I can't know your cranial condition. Have you seen Petit Bob? Is she getting used to Parisian life again? What would she say if she lived in Lyon? I'd love to get her out of her doldrums. . . . What about you? What are your plans? Are you still thinking of leaving with SIPEG? I'm counting on you if you can take me. The family got an earful when I talked about leaving again. . . . Goodbye, our darling doctor. Love you all.

Jacqueline Heiniger was delighted to return to France, for it was at the Warsaw airfield that she had met her future husband, Dakota pilot André Ribeiro. She sent a note to Madeleine:

> My dear Madeleine,
>
> Your letter has filled me with joy. I've left a lot of my heart in Warsaw, and if I give up the idea of planting my cabbages there, I still hope to go there, for example on one of those planes that will need a nurse. I was repatriated without detours by a sumptuous American plane that made a one-hour stopover in Berlin and left me at Orly the same day.
>
> France, my dear Madeleine, is the most beautiful country in the world, but it indulges in expensive, spoiled-girl experiences. It's rather worrying and even a little disappointing after the intrigue-free life of our little circle of friends.
>
> I give you a big hug, you've worked magnificently in Poland. To you, glory, honor and recognition. Many thanks from your friend.
> Jacqueline.

All the girls in the Blue Squadron were feeling blue. Some of them wouldn't stay in France but would enlist for other missions: Miche and Guillot to Morocco; Stiffler to Tunisia, Senegal, and Indochina. What did they miss about their lives in Poland? Surely, first and foremost, was the strong camaraderie that had developed between them. And the need to serve, too, to be useful. For each of them, it was impossible to do anything else, as Madeleine humorously expressed in a letter to Sainto: "I would so much like to be demobilized, but the army loves me passionately. Divorce will be difficult."

Anne, one of Sainto's daughters, told me that in her mother's retirement home, of all the furniture she could have chosen to decorate her room, Sainto chose only one item: the Red Cross trunk that had been with her since she'd joined the organization over seventy years before. This trunk contained, among other things, Madeleine's precious letters.

These were the letters in which Madeleine told Sainto about the various stages involved in her return to Poland. "The departure for Warsaw is taking shape," she wrote. "I had dinner last night with [the former French ambassador to Poland] Christian Fouchet, and he doubts we'll ever arrive. The roads aren't cleared, and he advises us to bring shovels, pickaxes, and plenty of food for the road. We have to be ready to sleep in the car blocked by the snow. . . . It's all very tempting."

She wrote again: "I'm off to London the day after tomorrow. I shall return on Sunday via Lille to see Abbé Beilliard. Monday the 28th: irrevocable departure for Warsaw. . . . May my moon and your saints protect me. If after all this I do not pass from the animal kingdom to the vegetable or mineral kingdom, I will go to the sun to tell you of my adventures."

Chapter 17

THE ACCIDENT

(February 13, 1946)

The news came in a telegram on February 13, 1946. Madeleine Pauliac was dead.

The next day, February 14, in the afternoon, Jean Neurohr, now a commander, wrote to all the girls in the Blue Squadron:

> I've just come back from a very sad mission. Last night, around midnight, we received a phone call telling us that there had been an accident on the road from Lowicz to Sochaczew, that a car had been completely destroyed and that two people, a man and a woman, in French officers' uniforms, had been killed, and the driver seriously injured; we were taken to Sochaczew hospital. And there, lying on two tables, was Georges Sazy in his colonel's uniform, and next to him, Madeleine Pauliac, in her pants, sweater and France Libre badge, her eyes wide open, her forehead covered with a little blood but her body intact, probably killed instantly when the car crashed into a tree. Yesterday, it was snowing, and the road was covered with a thin layer of ice. After rounding a bend, the car skidded off the road and slammed westwards into a solid old tree. A Russian truck found them. This happened last night, February 13, at 8 p.m.

Neurohr added, at the bottom of this letter typed on pink paper, "I was so happy to see her come back to Warsaw, bringing with her a bit of the perfume of the summer of 1945. And now I went to meet her, only to bring her back dead."

The next day, he wrote a second letter:

145

Dear Blues

I assume you received my letter of the day before yesterday, in which I informed you of the tragic and sudden death of Madeleine Pauliac and Mr. Sazy. We buried them this morning.

I had hardly finished my letter on Thursday when I was told that the two bodies had arrived at the hospital. The small hall downstairs had been set up as a chapel and guarded all night. Mrs. Longavenne, in tears, insisted on watching over the body. The next day, yesterday morning, at my request, the coffin was opened, as she wanted to see her dear friend and kiss her one last time. Dear Pauliac was lying peacefully in her uniform. Her face had been washed and her eyes closed. She had changed little and seemed to be sleeping a sweet sleep. Mrs. Longavenne placed a photo of her beloved Blues on her heart. This morning, at 11 o'clock, there was a funeral service at the Visitation Church, sung by the parish priest of Syska-Kypas. The entire diplomatic corps, the Polish and American Red Cross. A large number of wreaths, including one from the Blue Squadron. The two lead coffins were placed in a vault in the civil cemetery, to facilitate their shipment to France, should the families so desire.

At the end of the letter, one sentence seemed to escape from Neurohr: "My God, it seems so simple to die."

So simple . . .

On February 16, in Lille, Ducroquet wrote to Petit Bob,

My dear Petit Bob,

Thank you for your letter. I already knew the horrible news. You bring me certain details. Here are some more.

The accident occurred eleven kilometers from Sochaczew on February 13th. The body was taken to the Powaski mortuary, where it remained alone until burial, which took place on Saturday 16th at 11am. Someone had the kindness to lay a wreath of flowers on my behalf, and I was very touched by that. After the burial, everyone left. Only one person remained to visit the grave from time to time and have it maintained. If I ever go back to Poland, I'll visit this grave as a pious pilgrimage.

I passed the news on to Dr. Liber. My letter reached him in the Alps in the middle of his honeymoon. "Nothing could happen to her as long as we were with her," he replied to me. It's true that in the beginning, we saw some funny things. And it always worked out

well. Pauliac! She had written to me often since her return. She was
supposed to come to my place. I was waiting for her. She'd sent me
her picture. She wanted to see me: important. Why was it important?
Will I ever know? I owe her a lot, especially the most beautiful and
pure memories of my life. Don't ever forget her. She deserves it.

Goodbye, Petit Bob, and good luck.

I send you my warmest regards.

On February 16, Raymond Laporte, an employee of the French
Embassy, wrote to Henri Roux, in charge of the Eastern European
zone at the Ministry of Foreign Affairs. His letter did not have the same
restraint as Major Neurohr's.

> You will have already heard from our telegram about the tragic end
> of Sazy and little Pauliac. They were killed on Wednesday evening,
> some fifty kilometers from Warsaw, following a minor skid on a
> completely frozen road. The car we've just brought back here is
> crushed like an accordion, wrecked to a degree you can't imagine.
> Our friend and Pauliac probably died instantly. Both had broken
> spines, crushed rib cages and multiple other injuries. Only the driver
> is still alive, seriously injured but with a small chance of recovery.

On February 21, Jean de Beausse, former first secretary of the
French Embassy in Latvia and now France's Chargé d'Affaires in
Poland, sent a report to foreign minister Georges Bidault. He summa-
rized the circumstances of the accident that claimed the lives of doctor-
lieutenant Pauliac and commercial attaché Georges Sazy: "For reasons
unknown, they had taken a detour via Lodz," he said. "The road was
covered with a light layer of ice and it was snowing a little. After taking a curve, the car must have skidded off the road." Having visited the
scene of the accident, Jean de Beausse had examined the wreckage: "The
luggage had been taken away, and the car must have been looted. Many
personal effects and papers were missing, as were two or three tires and
some files that Mr. Sazy must have had with him."

It was a formal letter, a bit icy, written in classic administrative
style. Just one detail deserves attention: the presence of Georges Sazy,
commercial attaché, in a country that had nothing left. His role was
important, however, because for months an issue had been poisoning

relations between the new Polish government and France: the question of nationalized French property.

Before the war, France had been the leading foreign investor in Poland, accounting for over 26 percent of all foreign assets. Nothing was reimbursed or returned. Early on, in the spring of 1945, the authorities refused visas to a group representing French interests. Then, on January 3, 1946, a nationalization decree was issued, covering all companies, including foreign ones. France, however, did not intend to accept this action and demanded compensation.

It was a delicate matter to negotiate. The value of the companies had to be estimated, and the communist government had to be persuaded to pay. Georges Sazy had taken a hard line on this issue, which concerned him insofar as he represented France's commercial interests, or was his position a diplomatic blunder? "French capital will not flow to Poland because I can't be asked that it go someplace where it has been expropriated," he declared. What is certain is that France wanted to take advantage of the negotiation of new diplomatic agreements between the two countries to settle the matter. Given the situation, it is conceivable that the deaths were not an accident, but an operation undertaken by the communist government to forestall any negotiations regarding compensation for the expropriated French properties. Madeleine, in this hypothesis, might have been just an incidental casualty, not the target.

Of course, it's also conceivable that the accident was just that, an accident. Still, as the months went by, other hypotheses were formulated, especially as inconsistencies in the official accounts came to light. According to the Polish *gendarmes*, the car hit a mine. According to witnesses, it was ambushed. According to local farmers, the bodies were found naked. Some suspected an NKVD operation. But how can we know whether any of this is true, given that the truth behind the Iron Curtain has always been malleable?

Back in Villeneuve-sur-Lot, the accepted hypothesis was that the car had hit a mine, and, while there were certainly mines left over from the war, for one to be hit in the middle of a well-traveled road seems strange and perhaps suspicious. My godmother, a close friend of my mother's and of Madeleine's, always told me that Madeleine's body had been found naked because her clothes had been stolen. At the time, of course, I didn't think to ask her what supported her thesis. Was it just what my mother had told her? Was there any additional information? The local newspaper in Villeneve, in a eulogy to Madeleine published at the time, reported that the car was "blown up by a mine." "Villeneuve weeps today over the loss of one of its greatest and most noble figures," the paper wrote.

Certainly, there is reason to suspect foul play in Madeleine's death. In 2020, a long investigative article in the German weekly *Der Spiegel* found that Madeleine had been under surveillance by the NKVD since the day in April 1945 when she'd arrived from Moscow at the Warsaw-Praga train station, and this surveillance had never stopped. Her criss-crossing of Poland; the two hundred rescue missions she undertook over the next several months; her status as a witness to the murders, the pillage, and the rapes committed by Red Army troops; and the possibility that she would report to her government and possibly to the world on what she'd seen—all this would have made Madeleine a per-son of interest to the Russian intelligence service and perhaps a person to silence—permanently. Moreover, there was her trip to London just before her return to Poland, a trip very likely undertaken so that she could make contact with Poles who opposed the communists' takeover of the country. We don't know what contacts Madeleine might have made, but very likely, the NKVD did know. The reports that the papers being carried by Sazy or Madeleine were taken from the wreck is also a matter of suspicion. The two of them were traveling in an embassy car supposedly protected by diplomatic immunity, not subject to search by local police, so an "accident" and a "theft" of papers would have provided cover for what was actually an information-gathering mission by the NKVD or Polish intelligence. No doubt, local people could have discovered the accident and made off with the victims' clothing, their baggage, and the car's tires (though how many such people would have been venturing out on a cold and snowy midnight?)—but official papers, diplomatic dossiers? What interest would local people have in those?

Moreover, as *Der Spiegel* reported, engineering a supposed tragic car accident was one of the standard ways by which the NKVD eliminated opponents, suspected or real. Sometimes it might be a small explosive device placed on the road and detonated when the car passed. It might be a truck forcing a car off the road, or into the path of another car, or tampering with the brakes or with the tires. We'll never know for sure, but after her death, Ambassador Garreau announced that Madeleine had "died for France"—a designation usually attached to soldiers who died in war, like Madeleine's father.

Madeleine had two funerals. One was in Poland, the other in France, a few months later. Her body was repatriated to Villeneuve-sur-Lot, where it lies to this day close to the father she never knew.

"I pity poor Gilles," Stiffler wrote to another of the Blues. "To have waited so long only for her to disappear just a few days away from immense happiness."

Chapter 18

FAREWELL, MADELEINE

(July 27, 1946)

The hillsides around the ancient town of Villeneuve-sur-Lot are covered with fruit trees, and in the summer of 1946, the temperature returned to normal after a bout of scorching heat. The war had ended more than a year before, and the country was enjoying its first post-disaster summer vacations. Children were off to holiday camps, trains were running again, and the first four-wheel-drive cars were on the road. There were still shortages, though, and housewives were struggling to buy ration tickets for essentials, like milk and flour. The whole of France was singing "La Mer" (The Sea), composed by Charles Trenet, and soon to become a global sensation—"The sea, see it dance/playing along the shore." The song struck a nerve even in Villeneuve-sur-Lot, where the Atlantic was 197 kilometers away, but it didn't matter. Charles Trenet made hearts dance.

The remains of Madeleine Pauliac arrived by train in Villeneuve on July 27, 1946, a day of sadness. The whole town was mobilized for the funeral. The mayor, Léon Bonnet, who had returned from Germany, where he spent the war years as a forced laborer, made sure to do things well. Despite the wartime destitution, the windows were adorned with small French flags, and the public stood respectfully along the procession's route from Sainte-Catherine Church to the Saint-Étienne cemetery. A gasoline-powered Hotchkiss truck had been requisitioned to carry Madeleine's remains. The procession passed through the center of town, crossing the Lot River, and proceeded up the Avenue de Bias, a distance of three kilometers. The FFI, the French Forces of the Interior, the resistance groups integrated into the regular army as the Germans were driven out, had sent men in arms. Their uniforms were worn out, and their shoes, covered in dust from the powdery road, were tired. But the faces were serious, and that was all that mattered.

Madeleine was a child of the country, and the country mourned her. The catafalque was set up in the church of Sainte-Catherine, the largest in Villeneuve-sur-Lot. A bouquet of flags, amid a profusion of gladiolas, had been laid out at the altar, which faced a stained-glass window, showing a recumbent soldier guarding the tomb of Jesus. Gladiolas expressed love in the language of flowers, as everybody knows. The young men of the FFI, hands clasped in front of them, stood watch.

The Pauliac family was in the front row, with Madeleine's grandmother, mother, and sister, and Anne-Marie's husband, Jacques Maynial, who now ran the family's canning factory. After them are the town councilors and the most prominent families, the Raphaël-Leygues, the Cosse-Manières, the Monmejas, the Bégouins; then the workers from the Pauliac factory, and finally the anonymous, the unknown. The whole town was here for this final tribute.

All the women of the Blue Squadron were also present, led by Petit Bob. Someone was taking pictures. On one of them, years later, an unknown hand would write, "My greatest sorrow. Yes, for everyone, this funeral is an infinite sadness. A good woman is gone." The "Bleues" shared this sorrow, despite the joy of their reunion. When, in every corner of France, they'd received Neurohr's letter informing them of Madeleine's death, they were devastated. They agreed to meet in Paris before going to Villeneuve-sur-Lot, and when they did, their tears flowed, both from joy and regret—joy at seeing one another again, regret that Madeleine was not among them. This was the first time the eleven women had reunited since their return to France, and they reminisced, communed over the still-vibrant past, then boarded the train that slowly brought them to Villeneuve-sur-Lot, with Abbé Beilliard and Commandant Ducroquet. Here, their smiles gave way to consternation.

Madeleine's sister, Anne-Marie, organized everything, despite her despair and anger: despair at having lost her only sister, with whom she was so close, the person in the world she loved the most; and anger, too, at this hothead who'd left despite her family's pleadings with her not to go. At times, Anne-Marie wished she could see her and tell her

Figure 18.1   Madeleine was buried in Villeneuve-sur-Lot on July 27, 1946, five months after her death in Poland. The members of the Blue Squadron were there, their sadness visible on their faces, joining the entire city, which turned out to honor their local hero.

face-to-face what she thought of what seemed to her to be madness. But she sensed that her grief was leading her astray, and she pulled herself together.

She knew the deep bond between her sister and the "Bleues." She wanted them all to be there. "I will cover all travel expenses for the Blue Squadron and Abbé Beilliard," she wrote to Petit Bob. "If other people, apart from the Blue Squadron, should come from Warsaw, if you deem it appropriate, take charge of the expense; you don't need to ask me." This was her wonderful loyalty to her sister.

Abbé Beilliard took the pulpit, visibly moved: he himself had been a prisoner for five years and had returned from Germany ill, but now he'd come down from his home, a village in France's northeast called Bruay-en-Artois near Lille, to be with Madeleine. The months he'd spent with her, "over there" in Poland, had left a deep impression on him. He respected her infinitely. The Abbé praised the modesty of Madeleine and painted her portrait, offering "testimony," as he put it, "of a member of the team who, following in her wake and driven by her, spent four months on the roads of Poland, East Prussia and even in Soviet territory, searching for, rescuing, and repatriating our poorest human brothers and sisters, the sick, the wounded, the prisoners or the deported."

He offered "the testimony of a priest who, in contact with this superior soul—and I feel it a duty of gratitude to say this—understood even better and experienced the joy of serving for the sake of serving, the joy of putting herself, without any ulterior motive, at the service of the suffering members of humanity redeemed by Christ, who had cried out to the world, 'Whatever you do to the least of these my brethren, you do to Me.'" This was the testimony of a Frenchman who felt deeply proud to have served and represented his country in a foreign land—because how Dr. Pauliac served there was the purest glory of France. It was making herself and France loved by bringing material and moral aid to all those, regardless of nationality—and they were many—whom suffering and adversity had painfully affected."

The words echoed under the vaults of St. Catherine's church. When Abbé Beilliard mentioned the Blue Squadron, the handful of women in white caps and gaiters looked up. When he invoked the name of squadron leader Ducroquet, the latter took a long look in the direction of the altar, as if asking God for an account.

"She was one of those who work without saying a word, in contrast to the many modern Pharisees who shout from the rooftops as soon as they lift a finger," Beilliard continued. "But it's our duty to express this gratitude, to say it loud and clear, even if our materialistic, business-minded age has unfortunately lost the habit of doing so."

Beilliard's pain came across in these words, as well as the despair of a man who, returning home after unimaginable hardships, found a society incapable of understanding him. Once again, it was the impossibility of making others see what stood starkly and obviously in front of their eyes, others who couldn't understand either the pain or the exaltation, born of the feeling of acting for the good of humanity after the horrors of the conflict.

Abbé Beilliard went on to speak of Madeleine's "exquisite goodness" and her death "for suffering humanity." Then he returned to the traditional vows, of eternal life beyond death, the words of Christ, and "the light without fading."

This moment of communion was also one of great emotion. The first woman to come forward was Mme. Pauliac, Madeleine's grandmother. Her face concealed by a veil, she clutched her missal to her chest, placed it on her chair, and knelt at the altar. She found comfort in communion, just as she had found a reason to exist in the family's canning factory. Anne-Marie followed closely behind. It was now up to her to take care of her grandmother, just as her grandmother had taken care of her and Madeleine for so long.

Mass was over. People got up and slowly left. Outside, the weather was gray. On the road to the Saint-Étienne cemetery, under a hazy sun, a cloud of dust tarnished the shoes and trouser bottoms of the FFI and, lingering for a long time behind the procession, covered the plane trees with an imperceptible film. The dust cloaked this vacation day in a veil, as if to signify that the brilliance of a life, after all, was nothing. Serge Maurien, a young soldier walking alongside Petit Bob, had his Lebel rifle under his arm and, with his cap askew, was trying to look out over the crowd. Who knew if among the people present there wasn't some collabo who had discreetly prospered during the war years? Petit Bob, for her part, had put on her sunglasses, masking her tears, which, nonetheless, were staining the velvet of her collar.

From every window in Villeneuve-sur-Lot, faces leaned out, women made the sign of the cross, and General de Gaulle's declarations still marked the peeling walls of old houses—de Gaulle, who had just withdrawn abruptly, fed up with the ambitions, chaos, disputes, and manipulations of the liberators and politicians. The Hotchkiss truck rolled slowly past the lowered blinds, the motionless spectators, the empty stalls. The large French flag, hanging from the vehicle's sideboard, waved weakly beneath the heap of flowers.

Crepe-covered drums beat *La Bassée*, the grave, mournful funeral march. Mourners awaited Madeleine as the procession entered the cemetery. She had once fought in the war in the "army of shadows." Now she was going to join them.

From this immense grief, and from all the ordeals they had been through together, the young women of the Blue Squadron were going to forge an incredible friendship and solidarity. They would never leave each other's side, united as they were by the strength of the feelings that bound them to Madeleine. In this, they would be joined by Beilliard and Ducroquet. All of them (except, of course, for the Abbé Belliard, a priest) would build their own lives, marry, and have children, and these children, in turn, would become friends. For years, a letter circulated among them—they called it the "*roulante*"—containing the news of all the members of this "big family." In Poland alone, the Blue Squadron carried out over two hundred missions, covering more than forty thousand kilometers, in addition to the missions they carried out in Germany and Czechoslovakia. Madeleine's report to Mme. de Peyerimhoff, director of the French Red Cross women drivers, underlined their extraordinary understanding: "I never heard a recrimination or complaint when faced with the most unpleasant tasks and the toughest missions. We were always in good spirits. The team spirit was perfect. The drivers and nurses were outstanding, and richly deserved the citation in the order of

Figure 18.2 Madeleine Pauliac, who, on October 10, 1945, received the Polish Cross of Gold for her "tireless work saving and assisting Polish children." The French Legion of Honor was awarded to her posthumously after her death in Poland in February 1946.

the day from Colonel Poix, head of the military mission, honoring them for the work they accomplished in Poland."

Madeleine loved her "Bleues"!

Even today, the descendants of the "Bleues" form a large family, a close-knit group that meets regularly. The circle widens from birth to birth, and the spirit remains. It is a spiritual heritage that everyone is keen to pass on, because memory is the strength of a people.

A black marble plaque is affixed to the family vault in Villeneuve-sur-Lot: "Madeleine Pauliac, 1912–1946, doctor-lieutenant in the 1st French Army, Croix de Guerre with palms, Chevalier de la Légion d'Honneur, died for France on February 13, 1946, near Warsaw (Poland)." Near it was another plaque: "Roger Pauliac, midshipman in the 88th infantry regiment, fallen on the field of honor at Avocourt Wood, defense of Verdun, March 30, 1916."

Chapter 19

AND NOW

For me, Madeleine Pauliac will always remain a mystery. She died before I was born, but I have followed in her footsteps on a journey that took me from Paris to Warsaw, in search of documents, photos, memories, and witnesses. I found official papers—her enlistment document for the duration of the war, dated November 30, 1944; her notice of transfer to General Catroux's command, dated February 26, 1945; the letter putting her at the disposition of the Ministry of War; the reports she wrote during her missions and those of the men around her—papers yellowed, faded, forgotten. There was not much to go on. And then I found this photo, where Madeleine looked at the lens, a serious look on her face, her hair parted on the side, her neck highlighted by a Claudine collar and a polka-dot scarf-tie. And this other one, on the stairs of the French Hospital, in the company of some of the "Bleues." And the one taken after her accident, where we see both her head bandaged and her customary look of bravado, Tschupp staring at her. Then there are the episodes from her life testifying to its extraordinariness, summed up, for example, in her posthumous nomination for the Chevalier de la Légion d'Honneur, which referred to her activities before her departure for Poland, when France remained under German occupation. The citation credits her for "working effectively, despite the danger, to supply the maquis, and also, in difficult circumstances, helping allied parachutists." To this, the highly decorated resistance leader, General Paul Dassault—brother of the famous aviation engineer Marcels Dassault—cited her "exemplary courage and devotion, which demonstrated the purest qualities of patriotism in the fight for Liberation and provided testimony to the resistance by French women to the invader."

During my professional travels in Eastern Europe, a territory I covered during the years I worked selling film rights for Gaumont Pictures, I saw in detail the world of the Iron Curtain, the closed universe in which whole countries were transformed into frozen entities where scarcity was felt everywhere and surveillance was constant. Later, I saw this world change, and then, in 1989, the Berlin Wall came down, and with it the rest of the Iron Curtain. This was the region where my aunt Madeleine struggled and where she managed, despite everything, to achieve almost-unimaginable things. In a Poland in chaos, controlled by the communist authorities, she performed a miracle.

By what means did she do that, under what conditions, and with whose complicity? I've partly reconstructed the story, mentioning the mysterious person inside the provisional government in Lublin whom Christian Fouchet bequeathed to Madeleine. This man remains unidentified, and yet, he was undoubtedly invaluable. A French speaker, he was able to provide information that helped the mission in its search-and-rescue effort and also to keep it informed of the political dangers it faced. But even with his help and the bravery of Madeleine and the "Bleues," thousands of French nationals trapped behind the descending Iron Curtain were not repatriated to their country, and I still ask myself today how many thousands of people still officially designated missing were taken against their will, brought by force to the Soviet Union, and died there, abandoned by their motherland? How many destinies were crushed by history?

Try as I might during my own trips to Poland, I was never able to find the ravaged convent where Madeleine worked to preserve the dignity of the nuns and to help ensure futures for their children. Who were these nuns? Where was their monastery? All I'm left with are questions and few certainties. Postwar Poland was swept up in the maelstrom of the Soviet empire, files scattered, documents buried in forgotten cupboards. While in Paris, I contacted the Polish Red Cross in Warsaw; it was part of my search for documentary evidence of my aunt's work in Warsaw, and of the devastated convent that Madeleine had converted into an orphanage. All I had was my mother's account of the story Madeleine had told her during that long Christmas night in

Villeneuve in 1945, when the two sisters had talked through the night, when Madeleine told Anne-Marie how the nuns had come to see her at the hospital, begging for her help, how she had delivered babies who were the products of rape, how she had created the orphanage. Because Madeleine was pledged to absolute secrecy about the whole affair, keeping it even from Liber and the others in the repatriation mission, she disclosed it to only one person in the world, her beloved sister, Anne-Marie. I always entirely believed Madeleine's account. And yet I craved some documentary evidence, some independent confirmation of the truth of the story.

The Polish Red Cross' response to my inquiry was disappointing. There were practically no more archives on the period in question in Warsaw. And that was not surprising. Almost nothing remains of Poland's era of invasion and destruction, except perhaps the heroic stories of a people passionately attached to their freedom, who, using old photographs, rebuilt the old city of Warsaw stone by stone.

But then some important material arrived from Warsaw. I had commissioned a friend, a medical doctor there who'd carried out on-site research into his own family, to examine what was left of the Red Cross archive, and it was from his effort that one of the pivotal pieces of Madeleine Pauliac's history came into my hands. It was a letter dated October 10, 1945, from Ludwig Christians, the president of the Polish Red Cross, to Justin Besançon, president of the French Red Cross. Its purpose was to honor both Madeleine and Dr. Liber with the distinction of Gold Cross First Class, the highest designation of the Polish Red Cross. But the difference in the citations describing the achievements of the two awardees, Madeleine and Liber, is crucial.

Regarding Dr. Liber, Christians emphasized the "solicitous and understanding help given to [his] compatriots," clearly a reference to Dr. Liber's treatment of the French nationals whose search and rescue was the object of the repatriation mission. But when it came to Madeleine, Christians used the different terminology, which we've cited above. He spoke of her "great merits and her assiduous work to rescue and assist Polish children." Not "French nationals" (though Madeleine certainly found and rescued many of them), but "Polish children"! This yellowed letter, stamped with a red seal, provided the missing documentary trace of the existence of the twenty-four children, Polish orphans,

POLSKI
CZERWONY KRZYŻ
ZARZĄD GŁÓWNY

Nr. ____

Varsovie, le 10 octobre 1945.
rue Nowogrodzka 49.

Monsieur le Professeur
JUSTIN BESANÇON
Président de la Croix-Rouge Française

6, rue de Lisbonne

PARIS 8-e.

Monsieur le Président,

J'ai l'honneur de vous communiquer que le Conseil Général de la Croix-Rouge Polonaise a accordé la Croix d'Or I Classe, c'est à dire la plus haute distinction de la Croix-Rouge Polonaise:

1/ à Monsieur LIBER CHARLES, docteur en médecine, pour son éminente collaboration et pour le secours plein de sollicitude et de compréhension portés à nos compatriotes, ainsi que pour les efforts qu'il a fait pour établir un contact direct avec la Croix-Rouge Polonaise durant les pénibles circonstances de la guerre;

2/ à Mademoiselle PAULIAC, médecin-lieutenant, désignée par Madame la Générale Catroux, déléguée de la Croix-Rouge Française à Moscou, à collaborer avec la Croix-Rouge Polonaise, en vertu de ses grands mérites et de son travail assidu pour secourir et assister les enfants polonais.

C'est avec un vif plaisir que nous accepterions la nomination de Mademoiselle Pauliac, si dévouée à nos compatriotes, comme déléguée auprès de la Croix-Rouge Polonaise, afin de pouvoir continuer notre collaboration mutuelle.

C'est pourquoi le Conseil Général de la Croix-Rouge Polonaise propose de prolonger le séjours de Mademoiselle Pauliac en Pologne.

Veuillez agréer, Monsieur le Président, l'expression de ma parfaite considération.-

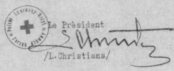

Le Président

/L.Christians/

Figure 19.1

Warsaw, October 10, 1945
rue Nowogrodska 49

Professor JUSTIN BESANCON
President of the French Red Cross
6, rue de Lisbonne
Paris 8eme

Dear Mr. President,

I have the honor of communicating to you that the General Council of the Polish Red Cross has accorded the Cross of Gold, 1st class, which is the highest distinction of the Polish Red Cross.

1/ To Mr. CHARLES LIBER, doctor of medicine, for his outstanding cooperation and for his help, so full of concern and understanding for our compatriotes, as well as for the efforts he has made to establish contact with the Polish Red Cross during the painful circumstances of the war.

2/ To Mademoiselle PAULIAC, medical lieutenant, designated by Madame General Catroux, delegate of the French Red Cross in Moscow, to collaborate with the Polish Red Cross, by virtue of her great merit and her assiduous efforts to rescue and assist Polish children.

It is with great pleasure that we accept the nomination of Mademoiselle Pauliac, so devoted to our compatriots, as a delegate of the Polish Red Cross, so that we may be able to continue our mutual collaboration.

It is for that reason that the General Council of the Polish Red Cross proposes to prolong the sojourn of Mademoiselle Pauliac in Poland.

Please accept, Mr. President, the expression of my perfect consideration.

The President
signed
L. Christians

exfiltrated to France! All of a sudden, it would seem, the Polish nuns whom Madeleine helped were making a recorded entry into history! Madeleine's official role as head of the mission to repatriate the French and as head physician at the French Hospital in Warsaw had nothing to do with Polish children. The ones she rescued were the nuns' babies and the Warsaw orphans taken in by the sisters' orphanage, including, we can assume, the twenty-four who were evacuated to France.

Little by little, the pieces of the puzzle fell into place.

Mr. Christians and Madeleine knew each other well, not least from their joint expedition to Danzig. It was on that trip, moreover, that Madeleine first came into contact with Polish nuns and began to know and understand the rapine that so many of them had suffered. As we've seen, Arthur Bliss Lane, the US ambassador, was deeply affected by the plight of the civilian population. Photographs show him in the streets of Warsaw, on foot, contemplating the disaster. In his book, *I Saw Poland Betrayed*, he expressed his indignation and disappointment at the country's abandonment to the communist bloc. In Warsaw's small community of Westerners, everyone knew everyone else, and it is well-known that Bliss Lane got into trouble with the Soviet authorities for helping to evacuate people.

It seems evident that these three people—Madeleine, Christians, and Bliss Lane—organized themselves to ensure the future of "Polish children" caught up in the turmoil of events. The Red Cross letter is testimony to the actions they took, which were entirely separate from their official duties.

The nuns whom Madeleine treated are long dead, but their children, or perhaps their children's children, are somewhere among us. As the last witnesses to a history within a much-larger history of the tumult that accompanied the end of World War II and the birth of the world order afterward, they might not know where they came from. Or perhaps this book will give them a few keys, help them to see the connection between them and Madeleine Pauliac, who did so much to enable them to live.

When I was in Warsaw some time ago, from my hotel window, in the gray of the morning, I seemed to see Madeleine and the little ones hand in hand. When I go to Villeneuve-sur-Lot, I never fail to salute, with a heavy heart, the great hundred-year-old cedar that stands on the way to the cemetery.

In summer, there are little blue flowers all around.

Appendix One

THE ABBEY BEILLIARD'S SPEECH

Speech delivered on July 27, 1946, by Father Paul Beilliard, Église Sainte-Catherine de Villeneuve-sur-Lot:

My brothers in Christ,

I commend to your fervent prayers, to your religious memory, Madeleine Pauliac, medical doctor, who died accidentally in the service of others, died for France. I have deliberately stripped my recommendation of all the titles I could no doubt have listed after this name, already so full of prestige for those who have had the good fortune to live with her and take part in all her overflowing activities in the service of others.

I never knew anything about her other than her simple name and the fact that she was a doctor—I never heard her enumerate the distinctions she had received.

I already have much to forgive myself regarding she whom we are mourning today, who was the first to be astonished that anyone could ever speak of her, and who would, with a certain disdainful abruptness, express her astonishment to me with all the frankness of her heart every time one or another took the liberty of praising her work.

But I have no pretension other than to give my words the sole value of a testimony, the testimony of a team member who, in her wake and driven by her, spent four months on the roads of Poland, East Prussia, and even Soviet territory, searching for, rescuing, and repatriating our poorest human brothers and sisters, the sick, the wounded, the prisoners, and deportees.

The testimony of a priest who, through contact with this superior soul—and I am duty-bound to say this loud and clear—understood even better and experienced the joy of serving for the sake of serving, the joy of putting herself, without any ulterior motive, at the service of the suffering members of humanity redeemed by Christ, who had cried out to the world: "What you do to the least of My people, you do to Me."

The testimony of a Frenchman who deeply felt the pride of serving and representing his country in a foreign land, because Dr. Pauliac was serving the purest glory of France, that of making herself and France loved, by providing material and moral assistance to all those, regardless of nationality—and there were many of them—who had been painfully affected by suffering and adversity.

And I'd like the whole of France to know it, and all French people to be proud of Madeleine Pauliac, who expected absolutely nothing, no reward, not even an acknowledgment of the splendid job she was doing.

She was one of those who work without saying a word, in contrast to the modern Pharisees, who shout from the rooftops the moment they lift a finger.

But it's our duty to express this gratitude, to say it loud and clear, even if our materialistic, business-minded age has unfortunately lost the habit of doing so.

The Church has always wanted its best children, those who, without calculation or self-reflection, gave themselves completely to the service of God and neighbor, to serve as a model and comfort to all those who follow them in the struggle of life. God will not hold it against me to recall the lesson that Madeleine Pauliac unintentionally taught us in her all-too-short life.

I hope that a more authoritative and affectionate pen will one day write this lesson for us. It will remind us of the incredible intrepidity and strength of will that resided in this soul, and also in this body, which beneath its apparent fragility was compelled to put itself at the service of others to the point of death.

My dear Commandant Ducroquet, dear Blue Squadron, you will have a beautiful, golden legend to write and splendid examples of this intrepidity to remind us of.

The days when, in Kawechinska's uncomfortable—and that's putting it mildly—building, Dr. Pauliac set about treating and bandaging the wounded and sick day and night.

In the days following our team's first serious accident, Madeleine Pauliac, suffering from a fractured skull, gave herself injections that calmed her suffering for a moment, just long enough for her to get up and treat all the physical ailments of the lamentable convoy of compatriots from Russia.

The day when, smiling as ever, she risked the most serious abuse, crossing and taking us with her across a jealously guarded border, with the sole aim of finding out whether French nationals were waiting on that side, too, for the care and, above all, the immense joy of an easier repatriation. And yet, what an admirable, exquisite, and gentle kindness in a soul that outwardly could appear so harsh, especially when it had to overcome the harassments of a loveless administration.

It was an exquisite kindness that made her disdain all feminine attire so she could be more ready to serve others. An exquisite kindness that made her set off without ever speaking of fatigue, day and night, on all the dusty roads of Poland, from the moment she knew that even one sick person needed her.

An exquisite kindness that made her give her friendship without return, a friendship that death does not break. An exquisite kindness that made her discern, with all her feminine sensitivity—I don't mean sentimentality; that word would be an insult to her—true devotion, that which went to the very end of self-sacrifice without seeking any reward other than the pure joy of serving.

And Madeleine Pauliac had undoubtedly found, in our fervent and simple masses, celebrated on Sundays during our open-air excursions or in poor abandoned houses, the strength to put into practice another of Christ's words: "There is no greater testimony to love than to lay down one's life for those one loves."

Dr. Pauliac died in the service of suffering humanity.

Dr. Pauliac died for France.

May the lesson of this life remain beyond death, which for us is only the passage to a better life.

Grant her eternal life, O Lord, and let perpetual light ever shine on her.

Amen.

Appendix Two

WHAT THEY HAVE BECOME

- **Madeleine Pauliac** arrived in Moscow on April 7 and in Warsaw on May 2, 1945. She returned to France for Christmas. Died on a Polish road on February 13, 1946, aged thirty-four.
- **Gilles Saint-Vincent**: destiny unknown.
- **Commandant Ducroquet** and **Abbé Beilliard** remained close friends of the Blue Squadron members, attending their friendly meetings right up until Beilliard passed away in 1978. (The date of Ducroquet's death is unknown.)
- **Charles Liber** succeeded his father as country doctor in Walincourt. He died on January 1, 1993. His son Benoît succeeded him.
- **Simone Saint-Olive**, **Sainto**, was born on April 3, 1921. She married and had two daughters. She died in Lyon on July 1, 2017, at the age of ninety-six. In a speech at her burial, at her family's request, Philippe Maynial, the author of this book, recounted the times Sainto spent in Poland during the war, a story that some of her friends were hearing for the first time.
- **Claude**, the young man whom Sainto found as a Buchenwald survivor, returned to France and built a new life. Two decades later, Simone's daughter married Claude's son, and Simone and her husband became grandparents.
- **Jeanine Robert**—**Petit Bob**—was born on May 19, 1923. She married and had four sons. She was deeply affected by the months she spent with the Blue Squadron and helped to maintain the ties that bound them all together. She passed away on November 6, 2011.

- **Aline Tschupp** was born on April 25, 1916. At the end of the war, she remained with the Red Cross for a further two years. She married and had two daughters. She died as a result of a road accident on February 8, 1986.
- Early in January 1946, **Jacqueline Heiniger** and **André Ribeiro**, the Dakota pilot whom she kissed one day on the steps of the French Hospital, attended a reunion of the "Bleues" and others from the repatriation team. "Not entirely by accident, I found myself by Jacqueline's side," Ribeiro later wrote. They spent time together until "[I]n the beginning of May, I asked her to be my wife." They had four children. Jacqueline died on March 23, 2000, aged seventy-seven.
- **Micheline Reveron—Miche**—was born on August 19, 1922. After the war, she went to Morocco to join **Violette Guillot**, who had become a school nurse in a southern village. There Micheline met a French agricultural engineer, and they married. Violette was godmother to one of Micheline's five children. Micheline passed away on May 13, 2007.
- **Cécile Stiffler** was born on May 24, 1922. After the war, she continued working for the French Red Cross, first on vaccinations campaigns in Tunisia and Senegal, then as an ambulance driver in Indochina. Under pressure from her family, she returned in 1954 to France, where she married and had two children. She died on May 10, 1981, aged sixty-nine.
- **Élisabeth Blaise** was born on January 17, 1923. She died on September 24, 1991. During the war, she was a member of the Red Cross' Nord-Pas-de-Calais sanitary automobile section. In September 1944, she took part in the liberation of Boulogne and the surrender of three hundred Germans. After the war, she spent thirty years working for an organization in Nancy that helped women in difficulty. She adopted two children of her own.
- **Roger Garreau** died at the age of one hundred in 1991, after a long diplomatic career.
- **Georges Catroux**, a five-star general, was the highest-ranking member of the French army to rally behind General de Gaulle in 1940. He died in Paris on December 21, 1969. His funeral, held in the church of Saint-Louis-des-Invalides on December 24,

1969, was broadcast live on one of the two French TV channels at the time. His book *J'ai Vu Tomber le Rideau de Fer* (I Saw the Iron Curtain Fall) deals with this period.

- **Arthur Bliss Lane** caused a stir when he resigned his post as US ambassador to Poland on February 24, 1947, protesting the West's failure to stand up to Stalin in Poland. He died in 1956, still scandalized by Poland's abandonment, after publishing a memoir, *I Saw Poland Betrayed*, which described in detail what occurred.

ACKNOWLEDGMENTS

To Barbara Maynial, for her invaluable collaboration, and without whom this book would not have seen the light of day. To François Forestier, who supported me and shed so much light on the historical context. To Caroline Sers, for her effective help in structuring this story. To Amandine Le Goff, for her kind regards. To Pierre Dumont-Hautesserre, who provided me with a wealth of family information. To Éléonore Charrié, thanks to whom I found the "Blue Squadron kids." To Simone Saint-Olive, Sainto, whom I had the immense pleasure of meeting and whose moving accounts of Madeleine and the Blue Squadron epic were invaluable sources for this book. To Simone Kunegel and Huguette Rother, Tschupp's daughters; Hugues, Jacques, and Denis Watin-Augouard, sons of Petit Bob; Christine Navel, Sylvie Henri, Brigitte Flamand, Nathalie Flamand, Olivier Flamand, daughters and son of Miche; Géraldine Navel, granddaughter of Miche; Gérard, Claude, Pascale, and Michèle Ribeiro, son and daughters of Heiniger; Christiane Adolphe and René Cler, daughter and son of Stiffler; Anne Vanbremeersch et Sophie du Jeu, daughter and granddaughter of Sainto; Benoît Liber, son of Charles Liber, and Marylène Liber-Maderou, his daughter-in-law, for opening their family archives to me. To the children of other Blue Squadron members whom I haven't yet had the chance to meet. To Dr. Pascal Eechout, for his encouragement, research, and support in Poland. To Pierre Bayle, director and spokesman for the Ministry of Defense; Lieutenant-Colonel Patrick Rongier, head of the Military Personnel Archives Center; Captain Mickaël Molinié and Julien Roudière, from the Ministry of Defense's Delegation for Information and Communication. To Virginie Alauzet, head of archives and documentation at the French Red Cross. To my editors, Bernard Fixot and Édith Leblond, for their sound advice, and Renaud Leblond, with whom it was a pleasure to work and who shared his vast experience with me.

INDEX

Page references for figures are italicized.

175